"Vanessa Levin continues to share her creative, holis[tic] must have book for all teachers and parents of your standardized testing has attempted to erase develo[pmental] practices, early childhood educators need to teach the whole child and follow Levin's recommendations to *teach smarter*!"

Anna Arlotta-Guerrero, Ph.D., University of Pittsburgh School of Education

"The perfect book for early childhood educators who refuse to settle for the status quo. Levin's practical tips – embedded in her highly engaging and relatable anecdotes – make this a must-have on your teaching resource shelf."

Danny Brassell, Ph.D., internationally acclaimed speaker, bestselling author, and co-creator of theREADINGhabit.com

"Once again, Vanessa delivers a true gift for early childhood educators. *Teach Smarter* will help you understand the critical literacy foundational knowledge needed to create an engaging, authentic, child-focused classroom. You'll feel like Vanessa is your own personal mentor as she walks you through all the key points with her signature humor and understanding."

Matt Halpern, Educator and Presenter

"Vanessa's insightful and proven approach to helping young children build strong literacy skills in a classroom setting will not overwhelm you, it will invigorate you!"

Deborah J. Stewart, M.Ed., Early Childhood Educator and Author

"Teachers, whether new or seasoned, have questions about how to put current research into practice in their classrooms — especially when it comes to literacy. Within the pages of *Teach Smarter* they'll discover a wise, friendly mentor to answer those questions and demonstrate by example — one who is always available, right at their fingertips!"

Amanda Morgan, Writer, Speaker, and Creator of Not Just Cute

"This book is a must have! Vanessa understands what to focus on, and most importantly — what isn't necessary. She helps early childhood educators navigate early literacy with a practical approach that comes from her years of classroom experience."

Allison McDonald, B.Ed., M.S, Author of *Setting the Stage for Rock Star Readers*

TEACH SMARTER

TEACH SMARTER
LITERACY
STRATEGIES
FOR EARLY
CHILDHOOD
TEACHERS

VANESSA J. LEVIN

JB JOSSEY-BASS™
A Wiley Brand

Jossey-Bass
A Wiley Imprint
111 River St, Hoboken, NJ 07030
www.josseybass.com

Jossey-Bass books and products are available through most bookstores. To contact Jossey-Bass directly, call our Customer Care Department within the U.S. at 800–956–7739, outside the U.S. at +1 317 572 3986, or fax +1 317 572 4002.

Wiley also publishes its books in a variety of electronic formats and by print-on-demand. Some material included with standard print versions of this book may not be included in e-books or in print-on-demand. If this book refers to media such as a CD or DVD that is not included in the version you purchased, you may download this material at http://booksupport.wiley.com. For more information about Wiley products, visit www.wiley.com.

Library of Congress Cataloging-in-Publication Data

Names: Levin, Vanessa, author.
Title: Teach smarter : literacy strategies for early childhood teachers / Vanessa Levin.
Description: First edition. | Hoboken, NJ : Jossey-Bass, [2021]
Identifiers: LCCN 2021002143 (print) | LCCN 2021002144 (ebook) | ISBN 9781119698890 (paperback) | ISBN 9781119698883 (adobe pdf) | ISBN 9781119698906 (epub)
Subjects: LCSH: Literacy—Study and teaching (Elementary)
Classification: LCC LB1576 .L497 2021 (print) | LCC LB1576 (ebook) | DDC 372.6—dc23
LC record available at https://lccn.loc.gov/2021002143
LC ebook record available at https://lccn.loc.gov/2021002144

Cover Design: Wiley
Cover Image: © ANNA_KOVA/Shutterstock

FIRST EDITION

SKY10029112_081621

Contents

Acknowledgments

I am eternally grateful to my husband Tom; without his constant support, love, and unwavering faith, this book would not have been written. From walking the dogs to doing laundry to grocery shopping in the middle of a pandemic, Tom was as critical to the completion of this book as I was.

None of this would have been possible without my amazing team who enables me to continually learn, grow, and serve alongside you. Thank you for showing up every day to help teachers (and children) around the world. Jeni, Scott, Rachel, Lynn, and many others did an extraordinary job of keeping the lights on and the wheels turning while I was locked away in my office writing. I am so fortunate to have them on team Pre-K Pages.

A very special thanks to Jeni for her expert editorial help and Lisa for her keen insight, troubleshooting, and encouragement in bringing this book to life.

Finally, thanks to everyone on the Wiley team, who were extremely patient with me as I learned the ropes of traditional publishing.

Foreword

We optimize early reading outcomes when our students are participating and having fun! That is why all my picture books, including the original four Pete the Cat books, Groovy Joe, and the Nut Family interweave music, movement, and repetition into the stories. Teachers often share with me how the books have made their read-aloud time more exciting. But what they don't know is that the books were intentionally designed to facilitate and model joyful and engaging shared reading experiences. So, I began to seek out new ways to reach early childhood teachers to share these ideas.

This is how I discovered Vanessa Levin's blog, Pre-K Pages. I was extremely impressed by her joyful and hands-on educational materials and ideas. Vanessa clearly understands what teachers need, and they genuinely appreciate her. Even my mom, a former first-grade teacher, was blown away when she visited Vanessa's website. It didn't surprise me that Vanessa had over a million followers on Facebook.

With my mother's seal of approval, I reached out to Vanessa to see if she could help me spread the word about the importance of joyful and engaging shared reading experiences to help young children build strong reading foundations. She was happy to help, not only because she values the importance of emergent literacy, but because she's a true early childhood educator who also knows the importance of sharing. Vanessa guided me through the evolving world of educational bloggers and showed me how to effectively use social media to reach more teachers. Like everything she does, her advice was practical, loving, and spot on.

Since then Vanessa and I have collaborated on a few incredible projects. When I published my Nuts book series, she eagerly and expertly pitched in to get the message out. And we collaborated again when I published my Groovy Joe series. In turn, I've participated in two of Vanessa's online Soar to Success Summits, which helped me reach more than 6,000 people in each session. I am always happy to work with Vanessa because I know she is very knowledgeable, cares deeply about early reading, and respects all students and early childhood teachers.

This is why I'm so excited about *Teach Smarter: Literacy Strategies for Early Childhood Teachers*. This topic is so important and urgent! Early childhood classrooms play a vital role in helping young children become strong readers. Vanessa is uniquely qualified to empower teachers to help their students become confident and successful readers. You'll reap the benefits of her 20 years of classroom experience as a public pre-K teacher and Head Start teacher, as well as her 10 years of experience mentoring, training, and coaching teachers. Her perspectives and ideas are both grounded in research and real classroom experience.

The book reads well because Vanessa is an extraordinary communicator. She is a sought-after speaker at national events. And she's a rock star online via her website, Pre-K Pages, and social platforms like Facebook. These experiences have taught her how to be entertaining and engaging while conveying practical, hands-on techniques teachers can use right away. Vanessa understands that good ideas must become great lessons and activities to be successful.

This book will empower you to help your students strengthen critical emergent literacy skills right away and without costly materials. All future literacy learning is built upon these crucial skills, which is why this book is so important. Vanessa expertly guides you through highly effective techniques for teaching the alphabetic principle, print awareness, phonological awareness, and oral language. Her step-by-step process is easy to understand and implement, and she does it with a deep understanding of what it means to be in the classroom.

It makes me incredibly happy to think about what caring and motivated teachers like you will do with this the information in this wonderful professional development book. It warms my heart to imagine all the children who will benefit and from your newfound knowledge and understanding of early reading. I'm filled with hope knowing that you'll be leading your students down the right path toward loving books and becoming lifelong readers.

Be well,
Eric Litwin

Eric Litwin is the author of *The Power of Joyful Reading: Help Your Students Soar to Success*. Eric is also the author of the original four Pete the Cat books, The Nut Family series, and the Groovy Joe series. Eric's books have sold over 13 million copies, been translated into 17 languages, and won 26 literacy awards, including a (Theodor Seuss) Geisel Honor Award. You can visit him online at www.ericlitwin.com.

Author Bio

Vanessa Levin is an author, speaker, and creator of Pre-K Pages, one of the Internet's most popular resource websites for teachers of young children. With more than 20 years of classroom teaching experience, Vanessa encourages and supports early childhood educators around the world via her Teaching Trailblazers mentorship program. Her mission is to bridge the gap between Preschool/Pre-K and the world of K-12 education. Vanessa lives in Massachusetts with her husband, Tom.

Introduction

My time spent teaching pre-K took me to some of the largest cities in the world. I started in Seoul, South Korea, then Detroit, Houston, Boston, and finally Dallas. Aside from language and cultural barriers, the biggest challenge I faced in many of these situations was lack of community and support. I didn't always have a group of experienced teachers to turn to when I needed practical advice or a shoulder to cry on.

In South Korea, I lived and taught with a group of teachers who had vastly different experiences and backgrounds. My roommates consisted of a high school English teacher, a home economics teacher, a middle school teacher, and a French teacher. I was armed only with my education degree—which doesn't come with practical advice. The Internet hadn't been invented yet, so I was left with my two best friends, trial and error. It was in South Korea that I learned how to teach with nothing but my imagination and creativity, with a few classic games like I-Spy and Hot Potato thrown in for good measure.

In Detroit, I was the only kindergarten teacher at a tiny private school. Although I didn't have many peers to collaborate with, I did have access to plenty of professional development books, which I devoured. Sadly, these books were quite expensive and ate up most of my paltry salary. While I was teaching in Detroit, I learned how to translate what I learned in those professional development books and put it into practice in my classroom.

My next adventure took me to a public school in Houston where I was surrounded by four pre-K teachers with more than 100 years of combined teaching experience. It was a teaching nirvana and I enjoyed every minute of my time spent there. My coworkers had answers for all my questions and gave me full access to their supply closet filled with a treasure trove of tried-and-true teaching tools. Unfortunately, it was short lived when I became engaged and moved to Boston with my fiancé. My experience in Houston showed me that having a supportive community you can turn to for advice was the key to becoming a truly successful teacher.

Next, I landed in a Head Start program in the Boston area; it was here that I first encountered resistance to change. I was the new teacher in a well-established program, but I was the only one with a degree in education.

Everything I did and said went against their "the way we've always done it" mentality. It was here that I learned you can have all the imagination, creativity, book knowledge, *and* a community yet still feel all alone and isolated.

Finally, I landed in Dallas, where I was able to put down roots and really blossom as a teacher. I was encouraged to use my imagination and creativity, and I had plenty of pre-K teachers to collaborate with, adequate supplies, and access to continuous professional development. It was here that I honed my teaching craft, with better results each year.

At this point in my career, I began to focus on creating a solution for teachers who were all alone like I had been in South Korea, Detroit, and Boston. I didn't want any teacher to ever feel as professionally isolated as I had in the beginning of my career. This is when I started Pre-K Pages, my website for early childhood teachers. I started the website to provide information from a real classroom teacher's perspective and to facilitate communication and collaboration. The idea began to pick up steam each year as the site continued to grow and grow.

In the meantime, despite the professional development opportunities, coaching, and collaboration that were available to all teachers in my school district, I noticed a strong resistance to change persisted. I started thinking more deeply about why some teaching practices are more difficult to let go of than others. I listened to and observed those teachers around me who were staunchly against change. Over the next 14 years I hypothesized there are three main reasons that keep teachers from making positive changes to their teaching practice, despite an abundance of research available:

Reason #1: Mile in My Shoes Syndrome

Nothing will make teachers turn their heads in disdain faster than being told what to do in their classrooms by somebody who has never walked a mile in their shoes. Research alone is not enough to convince some teachers to embrace change. This is especially true if the research was conducted by somebody who hasn't set foot in a classroom in several decades or has never taught the same age group or grade as the teacher it is targeting.

Reason #2: Too Focused on the Problem

There is a difference between defining a problem and offering a solution. If not done properly, and with finesse, an argument for change can fall on deaf ears when too much time is spent defining the problem and not enough time is spent introducing and explaining the solution thoroughly.

Reason #3: No Practical, Actionable Steps

This one is perhaps the biggest misstep of any argument for change. When an argument for change is presented without any practical, actionable steps given for how to enact that change, it will be completely ineffective.

My purpose for writing *Teach Smarter: Literacy Strategies for Early Childhood Teachers* is to translate research-based emergent literacy strategies into easy to understand chunks illustrated by personal stories and concrete examples. Throughout this book you will find plenty of practical, actionable steps you can take to build a solid foundation for future literacy success for your students. My hope is that you feel a connection to my personal experiences, feel reassured knowing there is a community of like-minded professionals just like you in this world, and you'll feel supported as you begin to explore ways to improve the way you teach early literacy skills in your classroom.

Although my work at http://www.pre-kpages.com has definitely helped me communicate and create connections with teachers around the world, it's helpful only if teachers choose to visit the site. I believe a book is a more concrete, tangible way to reach readers. There's something about reading a book and participating in a professional book study that makes the content more accessible to the reader. I encourage you to read this book with your colleagues and discuss your thoughts and feelings around each chapter. If you're isolated, like I was, then you're welcome to join in the discussion virtually inside the Teaching Trailblazers, my membership site for early childhood teachers.

STEP 1

The Alphabet

Chapter 1
Next Time Won't You Sing with Me?

It was a sweltering hot August day, three days before the first day of pre-K, and about 20 anxious parents gathered in my classroom for an orientation session. The first timers stood nervously around the perimeter of the classroom, keeping to themselves. The seasoned pros, whose older children had previously attended our pre-K program, looked more relaxed as they mingled and chatted with other parents. After we reviewed the parent handbook together, I invited the parents to help their children locate their cubbies, the bathroom, and other points of interest in the classroom and throughout the school building.

As usual, several new parents rushed forward and flocked around me to ask their burning questions. I had been asked these questions hundreds of times before in my 20+ years as a teacher—questions like, "What time will the bus pick up/drop off my child?" and "What if my child needs help in the bathroom?"

One mother stood near the back of the line, holding her young son, Brandon, by the hand as she patiently waited her turn. When it came, she explained how bright her son was and asked him to "show me" by reciting the alphabet. Brandon quickly recited the alphabet with ease and even included "next time won't you sing with me?" at the very end—nice touch.

Beaming with pride, the child's mother said, "He knows all the letters; we've been practicing at home." I smiled and nodded reassuringly at them both and said, "That's wonderful! I can tell you've been working with him at home. Brandon is going to be an excellent student!" Turning toward Brandon I said, "I can't wait to see you on Monday, Brandon. We're going to have so much fun together this year!"

But did singing the ABC song mean Brandon had learned to name and identify letters of the alphabet? Or did it mean he had learned to memorize it? What does it mean to learn the alphabet? The difference between these two skills is quite large; it's important to understand this difference before we begin any discussion about teaching the alphabet. Rote memorization is simply the act of remembering without a deeper understanding. Singing the ABC song is rote memorization.

When I was in the fourth grade, each Friday, our teacher called on us one by one to stand up and recite a poem from memory, which she had assigned earlier in the week. I would break out in a cold sweat as I waited for her to call my name. For some students, the poems rolled off their tongues with ease, which made the teacher smile and nod. Others, like me, struggled to spit out the words as they stumbled awkwardly through the poems, fearful of the reproachful looks we might receive from the teacher.

If you had asked me or any of my classmates to explain what the poems meant, we would have stared at you with the startled look of a deer in headlights. We had no idea of the meaning of the words we had worked so painstakingly to memorize. Like those dreaded poems, just because a child can sing the ABC song does not mean he has learned the alphabet, understands what the alphabet is, or that he can identify or name a single letter.

True learning requires so much more than memorization. To truly learn the alphabet, young children need to be immersed in an environment that provides rich literacy, print, and language opportunities daily. They need to interact with letters in hands-on, meaningful, and playful ways.

HOW YOUNG CHILDREN LEARN

If you wanted to encourage a baby to walk, you wouldn't sit the baby down and explain, "This is a step. First, you do this, then you shift your weight to the second foot." Would you become upset or frustrated because the baby couldn't walk the following week? No, you wouldn't, because not only is it an unrealistic expectation, learning how to walk is a global skill and includes many prerequisites. Learning how to walk is a skill each child masters at a different time, as they develop crucial prerequisites like spatial awareness, depth-perception, balance, and more. Babies develop many different skills at the same time, and we need to be aware of all those skills and how they work together in the process of learning how to walk.

The very same is true when it comes to learning the alphabet. Learning to identify and recognize letters is not a linear process. Young children don't learn how to identify letters of the alphabet by starting with the letter A and ending with the letter Z. Learning to recognize and identify letters of the alphabet is a lot like learning how to walk; it's a global skill that includes prerequisites. Young children learn to identify letters at their own pace, just like they each learn how to walk at different times. Letters can't be learned all in one week, 26 days, or even 26 weeks (Piasta & Wagner, 2010).

Teaching with confidence and skill requires a deeper understanding of how young children learn. This is much different from doing what has always been done and using methods that may have worked well in 1950, when rote memorization was considered learning. Rote memorization is no longer a goal in early childhood class-rooms of the twenty-first century because the needs of our society have changed. The jobs that will be available to the children in your classroom when they enter the workforce will require vastly different skills than they did in 1950 (Dede, 2010). More is known now than ever before about how our brains work and learn.

Instead of memorizing and regurgitating information, learning the alphabet in the twenty-first century looks much more playful and fun. Instead of sitting at desks while information is poured into their brains, today's high-quality early childhood classrooms invite children to touch and explore. Teachers expertly facilitate learning by setting up playful experiences that will motivate their students. Each child is learning letters of the alphabet as they become meaningful to them, at their own pace.

Although there have been many changes in the education field over time, one thing still holds true—when we don't teach the way young children learn, we're setting them up for failure.

IS THERE MORE TO READING THAN LEARNING THE ALPHABET?

It would be so easy if learning the alphabet were as clear cut as teaching all the letters A–Z first, followed by teaching letter sounds and finally sight words—then voila, your students would magically become fluent readers. The truth is that becoming literate is an extremely complex process.

Research has proven that there are four factors that determine future reading success (Dickinson & Neuman, 2007):

1. Alphabet knowledge
2. Phonological awareness
3. Print awareness
4. Language proficiency

Young children need an environment rich with all these experiences, one that allows their brains to make connections between the written and spoken word simultaneously. We know that some children come to us with some exposure to, and knowledge of, these four skills, but each child is at a different place in their individual literacy journey.

In Step 1 we're going to focus on the first skill on this list, alphabet knowledge. We'll discuss the biggest pitfalls to avoid when teaching the alphabet; and read stories from real teachers who have transformed their teaching, and their students' learning, by following the methods in this book. These teachers are members of a supportive community called the Teaching Trailblazers, where they've been receiving my guidance and support as they strive to adopt best teaching practices in their classrooms. And finally, you'll be challenged to reframe your thinking about the role the alphabet plays in the process of becoming literate. Buckle up!

Chapter 2

The #1 Well-Intentioned Literacy Mistake and How to Avoid It

Don't feel badly if you make this well-intentioned mistake; almost 5 out of 10 early childhood teachers do. I'm talking about letter of the week, that age-old common practice that you may be familiar with from your childhood or your own classroom. Teaching one letter a week (or day) is teaching letters in isolation.

WHAT DOES TEACHING LETTERS IN ISOLATION LOOK LIKE?

Let's take the letter K for example. You've got a crown and a cape in the dramatic play center for king and a koala bear and leaves in the sensory bin. What do any of these things have in common? Do your kids even care about koala bears and kings—or know what they are? Sure, your kids may enjoy it, but is it the most effective way to teach young children to identify letters of the alphabet? If there's no context, it's not meaningful to the children. In fact, it can hinder learning when children are constantly bombarded with koala bears and kings for no obvious reason when what they're really interested in are their classmates and themselves.

Letter of the week looks great on lesson plans and in parent communications, but it doesn't follow the way young children learn. It follows a linear path—a path that can hold young children back when it comes to reading readiness. Teaching one letter each week or day may seem like a great idea in theory, and it makes perfect sense to most adults. You teach one letter each week for 26 weeks, and at the end all letters have been taught—mission accomplished. With this approach, you don't have to worry about the order in which you teach letters; it's already laid out for you, nice and neat. Add in a cute craft here and there for each letter and you might think you've got an entire week of lessons for each letter of the alphabet.

TEACHING LETTERS IN CONTEXT

But what if there was a better and more effective way to teach young children the letters of the alphabet? What if your students didn't need a letter-of-the-week curriculum to learn the alphabet? The opposite of teaching letters in isolation is teaching them in context. Teaching letters in context means teaching them in a way that makes them more meaningful to the children in your classroom. Introducing and teaching letters in context (Fountas & Pinnell, 2018), using fun, playful, and meaningful ways is a much more effective method for teaching the letters of the alphabet.

Letters and their names are learned much more quickly when they're not taught in isolation. When you, as a professional educator, embrace research-based, evidence-based best practices, you open up the possibilities for the children in your classroom to soar to new heights you never thought possible. Your students will learn so much more than just the letters of the alphabet: they'll establish a rock-solid foundation for future literacy success. When you know and understand the why behind the what, you'll discover an entirely new world where teaching and learning are more joyful, playful, and fun!

But don't just take my word for it. Here's an e-mail I received from Beth, a pre-K teacher, about ditching letter of the week after 20 years in the classroom.

I've been teaching letter of the week for 20 years. It was what I was told to do when I became a brand-new teacher. The teacher before me did it, and I remember learning that way when I was in kindergarten. I started to have second thoughts a few years ago when my school hired a new teacher who had her own way of doing things. She didn't seem to care that we were supposed to be teaching a letter of the week. I noticed her kids excelled at not just identifying letters; they knew some sight words too.

Meanwhile, I was scratching my head and wondering what I was doing wrong because my kids were not nearly as advanced as hers. I decided to swallow my pride and ask her how she did it. I felt scared. I knew if it involved more prep time or longer hours, I wouldn't be able to do it. I was already working as hard as I possibly could and prepping all weekend.

What she had to say opened my eyes. First, she revealed that she used to teach letter of the week too! She told me how she read the literacy articles at Pre-K Pages about not doing letter of the week, which inspired her to get rid of it in her classroom. She explained how it became so much easier to teach without letter of the week, and she didn't have to spend hours searching for letter crafts or cutting out triangles for dinosaur spikes. She sent me the links to your articles and encouraged me to give it a try. I'm proud to report that I've completely moved away from letter of the week now and my students and I couldn't be happier.

Now I spend less time preparing, my students are more motivated and engaged, and they learn and retain so much more.

CIGARETTES AND COCAINE

When I was a university student, I signed up for an elective course on a whim one summer because it fit my schedule. A random advertising and marketing course turned out to be one of the most fascinating courses I attended during my college career. I sat spellbound, mouth agape, as the professor regaled us with stories about the early days of advertising and marketing. That summer, when I wasn't in class or waiting tables, I pored over the course textbook, which contained photographs of early advertisements for products like cigarettes and soda. Obviously, I didn't end up changing my major or ditching my dream of teaching, but the outrageous claims made in these early advertisements fascinated me.

I could hardly believe that cigarettes and soda were once thought to be good for you! Medical professionals endorsed them, claiming they helped with everything from fatigue and headaches to weight loss and more. Products containing cocaine (yes, you read that correctly) were recommended for relieving teething pain in infants. These wild claims seem ridiculous to us today because science and research have proven these substances harmful.

Medical science isn't the only field that has made new discoveries and advances in the last century. Research studies are being conducted around emergent literacy every single day, but it's more difficult to get the word out about these discoveries because it's not TV newsworthy. When it comes to learning the alphabet, children aren't dying by the dozens like they did from secondhand smoke or ingesting cocaine. And that is why many early childhood educators continue to teach using the letter of the week approach.

ALWAYS DONE IT THIS WAY

One summer, after speaking to about 400 teachers at a national early childhood conference on the topic of how children learn the alphabet, I noticed a line form in front of the stage. As I fielded questions from excited early childhood professionals eager to embrace best practices in emergent literacy in their classrooms, I remember meeting and speaking with a teacher I'll call Carol. Here's what Carol had to say about teaching one letter each week in her preschool classroom.

> I've been teaching one letter each week for 20 years. It's the way our entire center has always done it. My preschool students learn their letters by the end of the year, and they have fun doing it. The parents of my students are very happy with the progress their children make in my class. I get many requests from parents to have their children in my classroom each year. The kindergarten teachers tell me they know which students were in my pre-K class because they arrive in their classrooms well prepared.

I've met many Carols in person over the years at my speaking events, as well as teachers I've mentored in schools. Their names and faces change, but their message is always the same. Did anything resonate with you after reading Carol's statement? So many teachers feel the same way Carol does. Let's take a closer look at what she had to say below.

"I've been teaching one letter each week for 20 years. It's the way our entire center has always done it."—As an early childhood professional, it's important to become a lifelong learner to further your knowledge and stay current. What if your doctor told you she had graduated from medical school in 1990 and hadn't read any professional medical journals or attended any continuing medical training since she stepped out of the classroom? I don't know about you, but I'd run fast and far away from that doctor and start looking for another one right away.

"My preschool students learn their letters by the end of the year, and they have fun doing it."—Fantastic! Having fun while learning should be the goal of any good early childhood program. But is there only one way to have fun? What if there was more to having fun than just having a smile on your face? What if having fun also included your students being invested and involved in the learning process? Can you imagine what it would feel like if your students were so motivated to learn their letters that they learned them all naturally, long before those 26 weeks were up?

"The parents of my students are very happy with the progress their children make in my class. I get many requests from parents to have their children in my classroom each year."—Wonderful! Having happy parents makes the preschool experience more enjoyable for everybody involved. If you ask the parents of the children in your classroom what their goals are for their child's preschool experience, they will most likely say they want their children to be happy, make friends, and learn. Is having happy parents and many requests to have their children placed in your classroom due to you teaching a letter each week? Or is it because you're a good teacher who creates a positive and inviting classroom climate where young children can thrive? Please give yourself more credit because you deserve it!

"The kindergarten teachers tell me they know which students were in my pre-K class because they arrive in their classrooms well prepared."—What does well prepared mean? Does it mean your students can sit and listen to a story? Does it mean your students have good social skills and can control their behavior? Or are your students considered well prepared because you taught one letter each week?

Is Carol a bad teacher? Are you a bad teacher? No, of course not. Carol, if you're reading this, you're an *amazing* teacher! If you agreed with any of Carol's statements, you're also an amazing teacher. All I ask is for you to keep an open mind and to continue reading.

IS LETTER OF THE WEEK OUTDATED?

You're probably wondering how it's even possible that letter of the week is considered outdated when there are so many programs, systems, products, and letter-of-the-week ideas plastered all over the Internet? The fact of the matter is that change is hard—period. Change is especially difficult if it challenges the way we learned and possibly even the way our own children learned.

To teach the letters of the alphabet effectively, you don't need boring work-sheets, a gigantic alphabet binder for each child, elaborate and time-consuming crafts or anything else. What you need is to understand how children learn these concepts and what you can do to support their learning. It's so much easier than organizing tons of worksheets or painting hands—pinky swear.

CHANGE IS SCARY

The first day back to work after summer break can be both sad and exciting for teachers. On the one hand, you dread the impending disruption to your daily schedule, waking up before the sun, trying to cram in time to shop for groceries, do the laundry, and cook meals. But you're also excited to see your colleagues, swap vacation stories, and catch up on all the gossip you missed. If you're lucky, you might get to spend a few precious minutes in your classroom moving furniture back into place before all the staff meetings and trainings begin. During one of these back-to-school staff meetings the rug was literally pulled out from under my feet and my teacher world completely turned upside down—or so it seemed at the time.

In the school library, our beloved principal stood in front of us wearing his favorite Hawaiian themed tie as the mousy vice principal passed out the meet-ing agenda. As the principal reviewed the agenda with us, something on the page made me sit up and take notice. There, on the third line of the agenda: "Mandatory Fire Code Compliance Training." As a teacher, you get used to hav-ing new rules and regulations thrown at you each year, but nothing good ever comes from a Mandatory Compliance Training.

We sat through line items one and two on the agenda as we waited anx-iously for details about the mysterious Mandatory Compliance Training. The principal sensed our anxiety and tried to soften the blow by saying, "With each new school year there are always a few changes, and this year is no differ-ent." This sounded bad. I braced for the worst. Finally, he ripped the Band-Aid off. The school district would strictly enforce new fire code rules this school year. Before continuing, he cleared his throat and glanced nervously at our entire pre-K team, "This change is going to affect some of you more than others." *Oh no!*

We held our breath as he listed off the items that would no longer be allowed in our classrooms. "Curtains, lamps, microwaves, mini-fridges, couches, rugs, upholstered chairs, stuffed animals ..." I stopped listening after stuffed animals. This was much worse than I had imagined! Before he finished listing these new rules, hands shot up all over the room as teachers peppered him with questions.

"What about my lamps?" asked Anita in a quavering voice. Along with a claw-foot bathtub filled with comfy pillows in her reading center, Anita used several lamps throughout her classroom to create a warm and inviting glow.

Clearly upset, Hannah asked, "Does this mean we can't put paper on our bulletin boards?" Hannah adored her bulletin boards and often won the annual Red Ribbon bulletin board contest. This news devastated all of us because we had been trained by the school district to create a warm and inviting environment in our classrooms. Our hard work seemed for nothing. We had to undo everything we had learned and start from scratch.

Realizing the meeting was headed downhill fast, the principal pulled up a website on the large screen, hit the play button on the Mandatory Fire Code Compliance Training video, and hustled back to his office, leaving the vice principal in charge. The video explained everything that would no longer be allowed inside our classrooms. My head spun with all the changes that would need to be made in my classroom to become compliant. I felt devastated about taking down *The Very Hungry Caterpillar* curtains my mother had made by hand for my classroom. The stuffed storybook characters I had spent years collecting would no longer be there to help motivate and engage my students. And the brand-new classroom rug I had held a garage sale to fund would never even make it into my classroom.

During a very dismal lunch that day, our grade-level team sat together and made a list of all the changes we would need to make in our classrooms. Although we had been told what not to do, nobody had explained why we couldn't do it or what to do instead. I felt so defeated I seriously considered filling out an application to work at a retail store.

I had to seek out answers on my own to discover the reason behind this new policy, as well as ways to make it work in my classroom without completely having to change the way I taught. Why didn't they explain the reasons up front and end with ideas and suggestions for change? Your guess is as good as mine.

WHAT TO DO INSTEAD OF LETTER OF THE WEEK

Unfortunately, the Mandatory Fire Code Compliance Training wasn't the first time I had experienced the frustration of being told what to do without having the how or the why explained. I've trained teachers in person from New Hampshire to California and Canada to Texas. I know all too well that being told what to do is the norm; having the how and the why properly explained is the exception to the rule. In *Teach Smarter: Literacy Strategies for Early Childhood Teachers*, I hope to put an end to this frustrating practice once and for all. In Chapter 3 we're going to look at the biggest precursor to learning the alphabet and we'll dive into how to get your kids hooked on letter learning and which letters to teach first, as well as breaking down the scientific research for you in plain English. Hang on!

Chapter 3

Where to Start with Teaching the Alphabet

It's 8:15 a.m. on Tuesday morning, and your students are gathered around the carpet, ready to learn their letters. You're so excited to keep moving through the alphabet! You spent all day yesterday, pouring your heart out teaching the letter D and you nailed it. Go you! As your students file out the door that afternoon, they all touch the letter D you've so thoughtfully taped to the door frame and enthusiastically shout, "D!"

On Wednesday, when you flip your chart paper over and write a big letter D with your favorite blue marker, naturally you expect the same chorus of excited little learners. But instead? You get crickets. It doesn't take you long to discover that only one child knows the letter D (and she already knew it before Monday). How could this be? You worked so hard on your lesson plans over the weekend, and you devoted two entire days to teaching this letter.

Despite the three hours you spent searching for the very best ideas to infuse your classroom with the letter D, plus the four hours you spent gathering the materials and setting up your centers, your kids still didn't get it. You've got dominoes in the math center, dinosaurs in the block center, and a super cute donut shop set up in your dramatic play center. You're so frustrated! How is it possible your students don't know this letter when you just taught it?

Having a clear, easy to follow plan in place for teaching the alphabet is a necessity. But sometimes, despite your best efforts, a very clear plan for teaching the alphabet can quickly turn into an uphill battle, one that can make you feel like you're rolling a boulder uphill. You push, and heave, and give it everything you've got, and then some—but it just won't budge. What if instead of trying to roll the boulder uphill, you tried rolling it downhill? Wouldn't it be easier?

When you stop working harder by trying to roll the boulder uphill and start working smarter by rolling it downhill, teaching becomes so much more joyful. When it comes to the letters of the alphabet, teaching smarter means understanding the why and the how of learning the alphabet. It turns out, before your students are ready to tackle letter identification head on, there's a basic skill they need to develop first.

VISUAL DISCRIMINATION

Before children can learn to recognize and name letters, they must have well-developed visual discrimination skills. Visual discrimination is the ability to tell the differences between objects or symbols by sight.

Teaching visual discrimination skills is a precursor to teaching the names of each letter of the alphabet. If you're trying to teach children who don't have well-developed visual discrimination skills to identify the letters of the alphabet, it's going to be an uphill battle. Without good visual discrimination skills, young children will struggle to identify the letters (Woodrome & Johnson, 2009). But when they have well-developed visual discrimination skills, there's no stopping them.

One example of a child who may need more time and practice developing visual discrimination skills is Joshua. When asked to identify the letter X, Joshua said the number four. More time and hands-on experiences are necessary for Joshua to build strong visual discrimination skills. Once you help your kids develop strong visual discrimination skills, magic starts to happen—just like it did for Amber, a member of the Teaching Trailblazers, my supportive community designed to help early childhood professionals hone their teaching skills. Amber says:

I didn't think doing letter sorts with my kids would make much of a difference, but I was blown away by how much it helped them the first time I tried it. I got some cheap cookie sheets from the dollar store and drew a line down the middle with a permanent marker, just like you suggested in your video course. Then, I gathered a small group of my students who were struggling to identify letters together. We started by sorting magnetic letters with holes vs. letters without holes. I was surprised by how long this simple activity held their interest.

The next day, we were reading a story and one of my students from that same small group started pointing out letters in the book that had holes. This was a big win because it was January and this child was still struggling to identify the first letter of his name.

Figure 3.1

The more children touch and manipulate letters, the more information they will retain (Baker & Jordan, 2015). Instead of just telling your students about letters and showing them visual representations of letters, try adding opportunities for them to touch, feel, and focus on the shape of the letters daily in your classroom. These daily hands-on opportunities will eventually transfer into identifying printed letters. This one small thing can help your students develop strong visual discrimination skills.

ALPHABET KNOWLEDGE

The definition of alphabet knowledge is letters have shapes and those shapes have names. Whether that's a specific goal for your school, program, or classroom, or a goal for a future grade level, all children will eventually be expected to recognize and name all the letters of the alphabet (Foulin, 2005).

As professional educators, it is our job to create a strong, solid foundation that young children can use to build on as they learn and grow. But you need to know exactly where to start and how young children develop letter knowledge before you can start working toward the goal of recognizing and naming all upper and lowercase letters of the alphabet.

Remember Joshua, the child who said the number four when shown the letter X? Although his answer was technically incorrect, he does understand two very important things—the first concept he understands is that letters have shapes, and the second concept is that shapes have names. He just didn't give the correct name to the shape he was shown. Instead of feeling defeated or frustrated when things like this happen, it's a cause for celebration because it shows the child knows two-thirds of this important early literacy skill! Now it's time to start rolling that boulder downhill!

WHAT'S IN IT FOR ME

Have you ever felt like a used car salesperson when it comes to teaching the alphabet in your classroom? Instead of used cars, you're trying to sell the alphabet to your students—but they're just not interested. There are dozens of other cars on the lot, each one more colorful and exciting than the last. There's the block center, dramatic play, and art—each one inviting in its own way. What's the motivation for your students to buy what you're selling? A good used car salesperson knows the secret to getting customers to buy. That secret is answering the question every used car buyer has, "What's in it for me?"

It turns out, using the names of your students is the most effective and motivating way to start teaching the letters of the alphabet. When you use the letters in your student's names to teach the alphabet, you're teaching in context. Using their own names makes learning letters more meaningful to young children.

They may not be motivated by the big letter R you just wrote on the chart paper or the brightly colored magnetic letters on the board—but they are motivated by their own names and the names of their classmates and family. When they take ownership of the letters in their names, it makes teaching so much easier—it's like rolling a boulder downhill.

Name activities are fun, creative, and often have a three-dimensional quality, so your students are engaging with their learning on all levels. What if that letter R you just wrote on the chart paper belonged to your student named Riley? With just a few simple, hands-on activities, your students are pointing out examples of "Riley's R" all around the classroom. Then they'll take that letter and make it theirs. In Chapter 4 we'll explore specific ways you can use children's names to teach the alphabet.

Chapter 4
Your Alphabet Questions Answered

Although it makes perfect sense that young children are more motivated to learn the alphabet when we use their names as springboards for letter learning, it can also feel very unsettling for those who feel the need to have a very clearly defined starting and ending place for teaching the alphabet. It's a big step to take if you're used to teaching the letter A to your entire class first and ending with the letter Z. Suddenly it seems as if you have 26 different starting places and 26 different ending places—which can seem overwhelming. This is why, if my e-mail inbox were to hold a contest, "Which letters should I teach first?" would win second place, just behind "How do you teach the alphabet?" When you let go of teaching letters in order from A–Z, it makes perfect sense that the next question you may have is, "If teaching letters in order from A–Z is not the answer, then what is?"

WHICH LETTERS SHOULD BE TAUGHT FIRST?

Before we answer this question, let's take a step back and look at what we now know. Learning letters in isolation by teaching them one week or day at a time isn't as effective as learning letters in context as they become meaningful to your students. My best advice when it comes to answering this question is to teach the letters in your students' names first, and most important, the first letter in their names.

For example, Riley's name begins with the letter R, which is a bit more difficult for some children to learn then the first letter O in Olivia's name. The letter O consists of just one line and it's also a shape. The letter R consists of a straight line, a curved line, and a diagonal line, making it more difficult to recognize than the letter O. Of course, the letter R is very important and meaningful to Riley, so she will be more likely to learn the letter R before her classmates. Using this same example, if you were to conduct a whole- or small-group lesson using student names, your lesson would be more successful if you used the O in Olivia's name first, before you used the R in Riley's name.

WHAT IF YOU HAVE SEVEN ANGELS?

The odds of you having 26 children in your classroom, each one with a first name that starts with a different letter of the alphabet, are about the same as winning the lottery. So what do you do if you weren't lucky enough to win the classroom lottery? How can you teach children the alphabet using the first letter of your students' names when you have only a limited number of students in your classroom who don't represent all the letters of the alphabet?

One year I had 20 students in my pre-K classroom, seven of whom had the same name—Angel. This forced me to get more creative in my letter

Figure 4.1

introduction because I had fewer choices to work with for teaching the alphabet. Although I didn't have many student names to work with, *Dora the Explorer* was very popular with the preschool crowd at that time. Dora quickly became a member of our classroom. I added her picture to a name card and placed it on our name wall, along with the names of my other students. We did the same with another popular character, Elmo. Although Elmo and Dora may not be as popular today as they once were, think about what your students are currently interested in and, if appropriate, you can incorporate those names into your daily alphabet lessons and activities. You can also use the names of familiar people in your school, such as the director or principal, and other workers your students may see daily.

A few years after Dora and Elmo became members of our class, I adopted a dog named Trixie. I talked about Trixie and her antics with my students, frequently using her as the subject of our shared writing lessons. It wasn't long before the children began to relate to the letters in Trixie's name in the same way they did to the letters in the names of their classmates. Soon, they were drawing pictures of Trixie going for walks and chasing rabbits. This led to many children asking me how to spell Trixie's name to label their pictures. We didn't have a student in our class whose name began with the letter T, so I made Trixie her own name card and I put it on our name wall along with her picture. It didn't come as a surprise when every child in my class knew the letter T by the end of that school year.

UPPERCASE OR LOWERCASE?

Many debates have raged in the early childhood field over the years, but none as contentious as the debate over teaching uppercase letters vs. lowercase letters. On one side, you have those who say that teaching young children to write their names in all uppercase letters is the best method. Then, on the opposing side, you have those who firmly believe that teaching children to write their names with the first letter capitalized, followed by lowercase letters, is the definitive answer.

Let's take a step back and examine these two stances more closely. What is it they disagree about? Did you notice the word "write" appeared twice in the preceding paragraph? There is a big difference between writing your name and recognizing your name. Writing the letters of the alphabet requires many different strokes with a writing tool, like a pencil or a crayon. Letters of the alphabet contain curved lines, straight lines, and diagonal lines. Some of these lines are more difficult for young children to write than others. Uppercase letters have more straight lines than curvy lines, and lowercase letters have more curvy, detailed lines, which can be more difficult for some children to write.

When young children are first learning how to write, they're looking at the letters, then synthesizing the information they see in their brains, and then finally transferring that information to their hands. Eventually they begin to make marks on paper—some of which may resemble letters, and some may not. All of this requires many different muscles in the body working together at one time.

The set of muscles we hear about most often when it comes to young children and writing are the muscles in their hands. These hand muscles are often referred to as fine motor skills. I'll leave the complexities of fine motor skills to the occupational therapists, but basically, how well young children can write their names depends on their hand strength and many other important muscle groups in their bodies.

On the other hand, recognizing letters, whether those letters are in their names or in the world around them, isn't about writing at all. Stop and look around you right now. What do you see? Chances are, you'll see some letters of the alphabet. Letters are all around us in the world we live in. There are letters on the boxes and cans of food in our cupboards and at the grocery store. Letters appear on street signs, road signs, and businesses such as restaurants and stores.

Young children are surrounded by print every single day. When you read books to children, the print in those books doesn't appear entirely in uppercase letters. It wouldn't be realistic to tell children to look only at the uppercase letters. So where does that leave us in the great upper vs. lowercase letter debate? As with many debates, each side is arguing about something entirely different. It's not really a debate worth having. We know that writing is a complex skill, and we can all agree that writing uppercase letters of the alphabet is easier for most young children because their muscles are still developing. We can also agree that children see both upper and lowercase letters in the world around them daily. As a professional educator, you must take the facts and use them to inform your classroom instruction. So how do you do that?

You can:

Call attention to letters of the alphabet in your classroom and the world around your students without worrying about whether those letters are uppercase or lowercase. Be flexible and responsive to the needs of your individual students by calling attention to letters that your assessment data show they may need more exposure to.

Figure 4.2

Create a print-rich environment using student name cards and labels throughout your classroom. The labels and name cards don't have to be all in one case or the other.

In your writing center, you can provide your students with name cards or written examples of their names in uppercase. Be aware of where each child is in their individual stages of writing development and be responsive to their needs by providing them with the tools and the support they need to be successful. Some students may be writing their names using all capital letters and others may be writing their names with the first letter capitalized—and that's okay.

HOW WILL I KNOW WHICH LETTERS I'VE TAUGHT?

Wouldn't it be wonderful if you could just place a check mark next to each letter of the alphabet after you've taught it to your students? There's something so satisfying about checking things off a list. Unfortunately, check marks don't translate into real learning. Children aren't empty vessels waiting to be filled with knowledge from the teacher. They're active, curious, and each one learns at a different pace. There was a time in our society when teaching was all about telling, but that time is long gone. Have you ever heard the adage "When we know better, we do better?" To give your students the high-quality education they deserve, you must let go of the misguided notion that telling is teaching.

Here's a question from Pre-K Pages reader, Lynne, that landed in my inbox recently:

> I love the idea of giving up the letter of the week. But...I'm nervous about how to apply it in my classroom. I'm having a hard time wrapping my brain around how to teach the letters if I'm not introducing them in order from A–Z. Am I supposed to teach a different set of letters to each child? That sounds like a lot of work. What am I missing?

The piece of the puzzle Lynne is missing is assessment. Remember that boulder I mentioned in Chapter 3? Rather than pushing it uphill, we want to roll it downhill, and the way to do that is to collect data. Assessment is how you determine which letters each child in your classroom knows and which ones they don't. When you continuously collect data about what your children do and don't know, it can be used to guide your instruction and make it more effective.

Have you ever cooked a new dish for the first time? After tasting the final product, have you ever gone back and made notes on the recipe to adjust the ingredients? You cooked it, tasted it, and then your taste buds provided you with feedback that you used to adjust your recipe. That's the purpose of assessment, to give you, as the teacher, feedback so you can adjust your instruction and make it better for your students. When you collect data and then use it to adjust your teaching, your students will be more successful.

There are different types of assessment, some more formal than others. Here's an example of how you can learn more about what your students know and don't know just by reading a simple story.

It was the second day of school and I had gathered my pre-K students together on our large rug in anticipation of our first reading of one of my all-time favorite children's books, *Chicka Chicka Boom Boom* (Martin & Archembault, 1989). I eagerly anticipate the first reading of this book each year because it gives me so much insight into how much my students know about the letters of the alphabet and literacy in general. The repetition and rhyme throughout the book are catchy, and the colorful illustrations help capture the attention of young children.

As I pointed to the letter "C" climbing the tree on the first page, Carlos suddenly shouted, "That's my letter!" He was pointing toward the book, very excited to share his discovery with his classmates. I had them right where I wanted them! Carolina, nodded her head and exclaimed, "Me too!" Next, Francisco, sitting in the back piped up and said, "My brother has one of those!" while James sat next to him, playing with his shoelaces. Not about to be upstaged, Lucy added, "I climbed a tree at the park!"

I live for these moments in the classroom. I glean so much information about my students from just reading a few pages of a book. I don't have to sit them down and ask them to focus on a flashcard. With just one simple picture book I'm able to informally assess which students have prior exposure to and knowledge of letters and their corresponding names. I can even tell which students may have little to no prior exposure to letters or books.

Let's unpack everything I learned from reading just one page of a book to my students:

1. Carlos, Carolina, and Francisco all understand that letters are shapes that have individual names.
2. They also understand that letters can hold meaning by associating them with their own names and the names of their family members.
3. These three students may benefit from being in the same groups during our brief, small-group lessons.
4. Lucy isn't afraid to participate and has good oral language skills. She may make a good partner at center time for a shy, quiet child.
5. James may need more time to warm up to the idea of school and books, and that's okay! Or perhaps he needs to be moved closer to me so he can focus more and see the book more clearly—time will tell.

I don't despair that James is playing with his shoelaces or that Lucy has completely missed the point. Although only three of my students have made the connection to the letters on the page and their own names, it is not my cue to trade in my teaching certificate for a job greeting customers at my local big-box store. Besides, we're only on the first page—the book has only just begun, much like the exciting literacy journey that my students and I are about to embark upon.

In Chapter 5, we'll examine the criteria you'll be using to define effective lessons and activities for teaching the letters of the alphabet, as well as some concrete examples of what those lessons and activities might look like.

Chapter 5
What Learning the Alphabet Looks Like

At this point, you might be wondering what teaching the alphabet without letter of the week looks like in action. And you're not alone. Here's what Brianna, another faithful Pre-K Pages reader, had to say.

> I'm trying to convince my fellow teachers to move away from letter of the week, but we need concrete examples of how to teach the letters.

Before diving into the concrete examples of how to teach the letters of the alphabet, you first need to identify the criteria you'll be using. You can use the acronym

HEART as a guide to help you prepare effective lessons and activities to teach the letters of the alphabet to the young children in your classroom. This list of essential criteria, in the form of an acronym, will help you determine if the lessons and activities you're planning will be effective for your students.

Hands-on

Enticing

A connection

Repeated exposure

Time for practice daily

Now, let's examine what each of these criteria mean in more detail.

HANDS-ON

When young children can touch and feel the shape of the letters with their fingers and hands, they're more likely to remember the letter name associated with each shape. One easy way to provide hands-on opportunities for your students is to use magnetic letters. These come in many different sizes; be sure to choose the size that is most appropriate for your age group.

Figure 5.1

ENTICING

Your students will learn more when they're motivated to participate in alphabet activities. The best way to motivate young children is to make learning playful and fun. You can entice your students to participate by providing them with opportunities to interact with three-dimensional objects, such as magnetic letters, in fun and playful ways daily.

Figure 5.2

A CONNECTION

One of the easiest ways to make learning the letters meaningful to your students is to use their names or the names of their classmates and family members in your alphabet activities. When young children can make a personal connection to the letters you're trying to teach, it suddenly becomes more meaningful, and in turn, much easier for them to learn.

Figure 5.3

REPEATED EXPOSURE

Providing your students with multiple opportunities to engage in hands-on, meaningful, and motivating activities over time is crucial for learning the alphabet. Research shows that when children have multiple opportunities to experience a concept over an extended period, and a variety of different ways to practice, they're more likely to retain the concept being taught (Piasta & Wagner, 2010).

Figure 5.4

TIME FOR PRACTICE

Allowing your students time each day to engage in those hands-on, meaningful, and motivating activities is the most effective way to ensure learning will occur. These opportunities can easily take place during your daily small-group or center time (Hunter, 2004).

Figure 5.5

Ask yourself these questions when you're planning your lessons.

Hands-on—Does the activity provide an opportunity for my students to touch and feel the shape of the letters?

Enticing—Is this activity going to entice my students to participate? Will they be motivated to participate?

A connection—Does this activity include ways for my students to make personal connections to the letters I'm trying to teach? For example, does the activity use the names of your students?

Repeated exposure—Will this activity provide my students with multiple opportunities to engage over time? For example, can this activity be placed in a center for your students to revisit?

Time for practice daily—Can I give my students time each day to interact and engage with this activity daily, either with me or on their own?

What we learn with pleasure we never forget.

—Alfred Mercier

At Pre-K Pages there's an entire section devoted to early literacy where you can find many other concrete examples that follow the HEART principle.

In the next chapter you'll learn how to evaluate your lessons using one simple method that doesn't cost a dime. You'll also learn how to easily tweak your lessons to be more effective, so your students will learn more. And finally, you'll learn how to troubleshoot any problems you may encounter along the way, so you're not constantly starting over from scratch.

Chapter 6
Alphabet Reflection

An important part of being an effective teacher is reflection. Effective teachers reflect on what went well and what didn't, then they adjust their instruction to meet the needs of their students. Throughout this book, you'll be asked to stop and reflect on your own teaching practice. I know you're busy and you may be tempted to skip the reflections, but I encourage you to resist that urge. Without pausing for reflection, you won't achieve true change in your teaching practice. The only way to break through the "I've always done it this way" cycle is to take time to pause and reflect. But what does reflection look like in action?

For the first several years of my teaching career, during center time, I called students over to my teacher table to participate in small-group activities. I had a checklist of student names and I randomly called out their names when it was their turn to participate. When I called their name, I was often met with objections like, "But I'm making a castle!"

I knew that center time was very important for developing many different skills such as self-regulation and oral language, but I also had to teach the concepts and skills required by my school district and state. I felt at odds with what was being asked of me and what I knew my students needed, which was play. I made my small-group lessons as hands on and playful as possible to entice my students to participate, but there were still a few objections.

During my daily commute to and from school I often reflected on my day. I knew what I was doing was working for some of my students, but it wasn't working for all my students. I felt stuck between a rock and a hard place, and I didn't know how to get out. Then, one day on my drive home, I suddenly realized what I had been missing.

This was a turning point for me, and ultimately my students, because it drastically changed the way I taught required skills and concepts going forward. This realization was a direct result of the time I had spent reflecting during my lengthy commute. Without this reflection time, I wouldn't have been able to make the critical shift from working with students during center time, to having more intentional small-group instruction at a separate time during the day. The result of my continued reflection not only improved the way I delivered instruction, it also improved student learning.

REFLECTION

As you begin to reflect on the information shared in Step 1, I invite you to stop and think about what you're already doing that follows the HEART method. There's no need to throw out the baby with the bathwater and completely change everything you're doing in your classroom. In fact, I'm willing to bet you're already doing some of these things outlined in Step 1. Pause for a moment and write down those things you're already doing. When you write your reflections on paper, they become more meaningful and help you see the progress you're making or have already made.

CHALLENGE

Next, I challenge you to identify just one thing you learned in Step 1 that you aren't already doing in your classroom. Choose something that seems "doable" to you. If you choose something that's a big departure from the way you normally teach, it may become overwhelming. The most effective changes take place slowly, over time.

SELF-ASSESSMENT

After you have made that one small change, stop and ask yourself the following questions:

How did it go?

How did it make me feel?

Is there anything I want to change or do differently next time?

TROUBLESHOOTING

I would be lying if I said that making the switch from working with students during center time to creating more focused and effective small groups was easy. It didn't happen overnight; it was a process that involved plenty of trial and error. It's normal to experience feelings of frustration when you're trying to do something new. Here's what happened to Sarah when she tried incorporating more hands-on opportunities for her students.

> I tried putting magnetic letters in the block center and it was a mess! There were letters everywhere and some got lost. My kids were playing hockey with the letters instead of using them with the cars.

Instead of calling this activity a failure, I would call it a win because Sarah tried something new and she reflected on it. She just needs a bit of troubleshooting and some fine tuning to make this activity work for her students. To troubleshoot Sarah's situation, let's revisit the self-assessment piece.

What didn't go well for Sarah? There were letters everywhere and some got lost. Her students weren't using the letters in the way she intended for them to be used.

How did it make her feel? She was frustrated.

Is there anything she could change or do differently? Yes. She could start by spending more time introducing the letters in the block center and setting expectations. One way she could introduce the car parking lot activity is to incorporate it into a small-group lesson. This way, each child in her class would have the opportunity to engage in the activity with her in a more supportive setting. During her lesson she could establish expectations and provide supervised time for her students to explore the cars and letters. After each child has had a chance to participate in her small-group lesson, then she could review it with the entire class and, finally, put it in the block center for free exploration.

Reflection is the key to affecting change in your classroom. When you feel stuck, I want you to come back to this chapter and go through the steps again. But it can be difficult to start making changes to your teaching practice on your own because change doesn't happen overnight. Embracing change is a lot like starting a diet. You don't lose the weight immediately; you make changes to your diet that result in gradual weight loss over time. If you would like additional support and guidance as you begin to embrace change, go to http://www.pre-kpages.com/TeachSmarter for resources that will help you become the most confident and effective teacher you can be. There you can join our free Alphabet Challenge and connect with other like-minded professionals. You can also download the free Literacy Essentials Guide, which includes all my best activities for effectively teaching the alphabet in hands-on, fun, and playful ways.

In Step 2, we'll focus on print awareness—what it is, why it's important, and what it looks like in action in the early childhood classroom. You'll learn exactly how to help your students develop important print awareness skills that will help them become successful lifelong readers.

STEP 2

Print Awareness

Chapter 7
What Is Print Awareness?

It's not unusual for each new school year to bring feelings of excitement and nervousness, for both teachers and students. This was my 15th first day of school as a preschool teacher, and I was anxiously waiting for my new students to fill the classroom with the buzz and hum of their playful energy. Surprisingly, they arrived in my classroom without too much separation anxiety, always a huge relief for any teacher. We were about 35 minutes into our day and aside from a few "When's my mommy coming back?" questions, things were going smoothly so far. The children had put their belongings in their cubbies with assistance and visited the bathroom, and I had succeeded in reading a short story from start to finish—a huge win for any first day!

I eagerly anticipated the next step in our day, which was introducing the bookshelf to the children and inviting them to "read" books for a few minutes. This may seem like a trivial thing to get excited about, but it allowed me to quickly see my students' understanding of books and how they worked. As I explained how to choose a book, sit down and look at it, and then return it to the bookshelf, one little boy excitedly asked in a shocked voice, "Any book we want?" After reassuring him that he could indeed choose any book he wanted, I watched the magic happen.

Another student, Ariel, made a beeline for *The Very Hungry Caterpillar* (Carle, 1980). "I know this one!" she exclaimed. She removed the book from the shelf, sat down on the carpet, and began turning the pages. Her actions told me so much about her level of print awareness. She held the book with the cover facing up, she turned the pages one by one, and she orally retold the story by looking at the pictures. This quick observation told me that Ariel had a good grasp on early reading behaviors.

Edgar approached the bookshelf hesitantly. He was more interested in exploring the other areas of the classroom, like the block center. He gazed at the books on the shelf for a moment before selecting a book with a colorful illustration on the front depicting a bulldozer. Then, he meandered to the carpet and eventually sat down next to Ariel. He put the book on the floor in front of him, but he was more interested in listening to Ariel tell the story of the caterpillar out loud.

When Ariel got up to return her book to the shelf, Edgar hesitantly picked up his book and opened it to the last page. Instead of turning the pages one by one, he brushed them with his hand and turned them awkwardly, several at a time. After shuffling backward through the pages, from back to front, he returned his book to the shelf and placed it upside down. He was mimicking the behavior he saw from Ariel, which told me he may not have developed many of the early reading behaviors she exhibited. I didn't despair because I still had an entire school year to help Edgar develop the necessary print concepts he would need to become a successful reader later.

UNDERSTANDING PRINT AWARENESS

The basic understandings of how books and print work are often referred to as print awareness skills, or concepts of print (Clay, 2019). For example, where is the top of the book? Where is the front? The back? As an adult, you might not give these things any thought when you pick up a book and start reading.

Although they may seem insignificant to us as adults, these skills are especially important parts of the early literacy process for young children. These important print concepts include:

Letters and words hold meaning.

Print is what we read.

Illustrations correspond to the print.

We read from left to right.

We read from top to bottom.

We start reading on the left.

One-to-one correspondence—print matches spoken words.

Return sweep—when we get to the end of a line on a page we return to the next line and begin reading on the left again.

Books have a title.

Books have a front and a back.

Books have a top and a bottom.

The author writes the words.

The illustrator draws the pictures or the photographer takes the pictures.

Letters and words are different.

There are spaces between words.

Punctuation helps us understand what we read.

Developing print awareness skills is a lengthy process that takes place over time. Each child will learn these concepts at his or her own pace.

THE IMPORTANCE OF PRINT AWARENESS

Before children can begin to read, they must first understand how books and print work. Considered precursors to reading and writing, print awareness skills are crucial components of the early literacy process. Young children may begin to develop print awareness at a very young age. How quickly they learn these concepts is directly related to how often they are read to and how often they interact with books and print—both at home and in the classroom. Without a good understanding of these basic print concepts, young children will struggle to become successful readers later (McKenna & Dougherty Stahl, 2009).

When young children are immersed in a print-rich environment that includes multiple opportunities to listen to and interact with books and print daily, then learning these important skills will become easier. These opportunities must include time spent listening to books being read aloud as well as time spent with books independently. When young children are read to multiple times daily and they have intentional time to interact with books and print each day, their awareness of print will become stronger.

PRINT AWARENESS PRECURSORS

Although print awareness is considered a precursor to reading, I believe there are some specific and intentional ways you can make learning these concepts easier for young children. Consider these skills the precursors to the precursors if you will. Before they can become successful readers, young children need to be motivated to read and to think they're capable of reading themselves. Having a clear plan in place to support the development of these skills will set your students up for success.

MOTIVATION TO READ

When I was a young student teacher, I met Kay. She taught second grade down the hall from the kindergarten classroom where I had been assigned. Kay had the most beautiful classroom library in the entire school. Aside from the usual books, there was a big leafy tree constructed with butcher paper in one corner, soft pillows, a floor lamp, and a luxurious green rug. The students in her class-room adored Kay and her magnificent library of captivating books.

Kay was retiring at the end of the year, and she enjoyed reminiscing fondly on her days as a teacher. One spring day, while eating lunch in the teacher's lounge, I overheard another teacher ask Kay if she would be having a garage sale to get rid of her massive collection of children's books. Intrigued by the prospect of affordable picture books, I piped up and asked the obvious, "How many books do you have?"

A few of the other teachers chuckled at my question as Kay replied, "More than I should have; I could open my own library." Then she added slyly, "Why don't you come over after school on Friday and I'll show you my collection—you can have first pick." I wasn't sure why, but I was suddenly reminded of the story of the Gingerbread Man.

That Friday, I eagerly accompanied Kay to her home, which was just down the street from the school. As we walked, enjoying the fresh spring air, Kay started telling me about her 28-year-old son, Kyle. The picture she painted made him sound like Prince Charming. I suddenly realized that sweet Kay had ulterior motives for inviting me to her home. Nonetheless, the prospect of stocking my future classroom library with affordable children's books was too alluring, so I played along.

When we reached her house, Kay led me through the front door, down the hall, and toward the back of the house. What had once been the back door no longer led to the yard; instead it opened to reveal an entire room filled floor to ceiling with children's picture books. The stunned expression on my face prompted Kay to explain, "Ten years ago, my husband said it was him or the books because they were taking over our entire house, so he built me this beautiful library."

Although I loved children's books as much as the next primary teacher, I couldn't figure out why anybody would want or need so many books. I didn't need to ask, because Kay started quickly explaining her reasoning to me. For the next 30 minutes she expertly guided me around the room as she took books off the shelves, explaining why each one was a prized member of her carefully curated collection. I noticed a common theme in each of her stories. She was describing how each book made her and her students feel and why. She talked about her books as if they were people she loved.

I was intrigued by the number of multiple copies of the same book she had on her shelves, so I inquired about the purpose. What she said next affected how I viewed books in my own classroom for the next 20 years. She patiently explained her thought process to me, "When I read a book to my students, I'm introducing them to what I hope is the newest member of their family. When a mother brings home a new baby, she doesn't keep the other members of her immediate family away from the baby. Instead, they interact with the baby and bond with it. That's how a baby becomes a cherished member of the family. That's why I need multiple copies of some books; my students need time to bond with them."

Having multiple copies of the same book allowed Kay's students opportunities to read their favorites at any time. Instead of reading a book and putting it away on a shelf, out of their reach, Kay was inviting her students to read her treasured books, which in turn helped her students become lifelong readers. And, just in case you're wondering, I didn't end up dating her son, but I did walk away with several new members of my own book family that day.

Clearly, Kay understood the concept of motivating young children to read. She conveyed her love of books and reading to her students by holding books in the highest regard and showing her students she loved them dearly. She also provided her students with multiple copies so they could spend time making the books their own and learning to love them. Although Kay taught older students, her philosophy can easily be applied to the early childhood classroom.

BELIEVING THEY CAN READ

For young children, there's a big difference between listening to a story being read aloud and picking up a book and believing they can read it. Often, young children see reading as something that only adults can do. When we create intentional opportunities for children to see themselves as capable of reading, that's when they really begin to exhibit early reading behaviors and develop print concepts.

One brisk November day after school, while I was working on student portfolios for upcoming parent conferences, I heard footsteps in the hallway outside my classroom door. I looked up and saw Hector's mother standing in the doorway with a very purposeful look on her face. The corners of her mouth were downturned, her brow was furrowed, and one hand was placed firmly on her hip...uh-oh! Her son, Hector, was a bright little boy who was always happy and eager to come to school. I was puzzled about why she would suddenly turn up in my classroom with such an unpleasant demeanor.

I stood up awkwardly from the tiny chair where I had been sitting and said, "How nice to see you; please come in," in my most pleasant voice reserved for special occasions such as this. Smiling, I asked, "What can I do for you today?"

"Hector says he can read!" she blurted out. The exasperation in her voice was palpable as she went on to explain, "He comes home from school every day and he says he can read, but all he's doing is pointing to words on boxes and signs. I told him that wasn't reading, but he said you told him he was a reader. Why are you lying to him?" I felt a sense of relief as I realized that this was just a simple misunderstanding

"I can understand how you might think that; please sit down and let's talk." I replied as I motioned to the miniature chair across the table. As I calmly explained the importance of environmental print and the role it plays in creating motivation to read, I saw her slowly start to relax. The corners of her mouth returned to their normal position and the furrows in her brow disappeared. Anticipating her next question, I quickly added, "There are many different steps in learning how to read, this is just one of them. Pointing to signs and words tells us that Hector is on his way to becoming a successful reader."

Remember Edgar? He needed motivation to read and to believe in himself as a reader more than anything else. Helping young children develop print awareness requires highly skilled and carefully planned opportunities throughout the school year. In Chapter 8 we'll explore some specific ways you can help your students develop these important skills.

What Does Learning Print Awareness Look Like in the Classroom?

Every October I looked forward to reading one of my all-time favorite books aloud to my students, *Mrs. Wishy-Washy* (Cowley, 1980); it never gets old. This particular year, about ten years into my teaching career, was no different. As I placed the oversized book on my easel, I said excitedly, "I have a surprise for you today. This is one of my favorite books ever and I can't wait to share it with you!"

Then I asked, "What do you think this story could be about?" Young children rarely need to be invited to share their opinions and several immediately shouted out the obvious, "A lady!"

I prompted them further by asking, "What do you notice about the lady?"

"She's got something on her head!" exclaimed Jackson excitedly.

"She looks mad," said Jasmine.

"She's wearing slippers!" shouted Frankie.

"This is one of my favorite books because it's funny. Do you like funny stories?" I asked. Many of the children nodded affirmatively, while others shouted out in agreement.

Next, I pulled out my trusty pointer, the blue one, with the little white hand and the pointed finger on the end. (Pointers always make reading so much more fun, for both the teacher and the students.) I pointed carefully to each word on the cover of the big book with my pointer. As I pointed, I explained, "This is the title. The title is the name of the story. The title of this story is *Mrs. Wishy-Washy*."

"Have you ever heard of somebody named Mrs. Wishy-Washy before?" I asked. Most children agreed that they had never heard the name before, but one little boy sitting to my left asked, "What's a Wishy-Washy?" I couldn't have asked for a more perfect segue. "Let's find out!" I said excitedly.

As I turned the pages of the book, the children noticed and discussed the pictures on each page. They quickly discovered the story was about a farm and farm animals, so I asked, "Have you ever been to a farm before?" This question elicited lots of excited responses about farms and animals they had seen, some of which they had experienced in person and some they had experienced only on a screen.

When we were finished looking at the pictures in the book, one observant little girl piped up and said, "But you didn't read the story!" I had them right where I wanted them! I feigned surprise and said innocently, "Oh my, you're right! Let's read the words with my pointer."

This time, I pointed to the words on each page of the big book with my pointer as we chanted "wishy-washy, wishy-washy" in unison throughout the story. As we chanted together, I invited the children to pretend they were scrubbing the animals from the story, just like the main character. When I reached the last page and closed the book, I said, "The end."

Then, we launched into a brief but lively discussion about why they thought Mrs. Wishy-Washy was giving the animals a bath. Finally, I said, "Who liked this story?," which elicited a loud chorus of "Me! Me! Me!" I held up a regular size version of the book and said, "If you liked this story you can find it over here in our classroom library." I walked with the book over to our cozy book area and placed it on the shelf as the children watched.

If you're wondering how this lesson relates to developing print awareness, let's look at it more closely. Remember the list of print concepts from Chapter 7? While pointing to the words on the pages of the big book with the pointer, we demonstrated that **letters and words hold meaning** and **print is what we read**. We defined the word **title**, and we discussed the **title of the book**. When teaching print concepts, it's important to use enlarged text, such as the text in big books, so young children can see more clearly as you read and demonstrate.

The simple act of using the pointer to read the words in the big book called attention to the following concepts:

We read from **left to right**.

We read from **top to bottom**.

We start reading on the left side of each page

One-to-one correspondence—print matches spoken words.

Return sweep—when we get to the end of a line on a page we return to the next line and begin reading on the left again.

There's so much more learning that took place during this lesson—we've barely scratched the surface. One aspect of this lesson we haven't addressed yet is motivation to read. Remember Kay and her love for books? This lesson used Kay's theory of introducing a book to her students as cherished members of their family. But this lesson is far from over—now the children need time to bond with the book. What does the process of bonding with a book look like in action?

When I walked the book over to our classroom library at the end of the lesson, I was inviting my students to spend more time with the book on their own. It was my favorite book, and now I was sharing it with them and inviting them to bond with it. But the mere act of placing the book on the shelf isn't going to guarantee children will read it if it's a choice only during center time. Think of all the competition poor Mrs. Wishy-Washy has during center time: she takes a back seat to the more exciting centers like blocks or dramatic play!

What if, instead of choosing between Mrs. Wishy-Washy and the blocks center, there was a dedicated "reading time" during each day? This time is set aside for enjoying books for pleasure, without competition from the other, more irresistible centers. In my own classroom, I called this BEAR time, or Be Excited About Reading. This time, although very brief, is also a powerful tool that can

Figure 8.1

Figure 8.2

help boost your students' print awareness skills and allows them to bond with their own personal favorites.

Before they can start decoding words and get started with "real" reading, they first need to love reading and be motivated to read. It can be tricky to manage a dedicated reading time with young children at first, but once you incorporate it into your daily classroom routine and your students get the hang of it, it will quickly become the highlight of their day.

The books in your classroom don't have to be contained in just one area, such as the classroom library. Instead, place books in each center or interest area. Books about vehicles and construction are perfect for your block center. Books about counting and other math skills are ideal for your math center. You can even put books about families, babies, food, and more in your dramatic play area.

When you place books in your centers it's important to explicitly call attention to their purpose. For example, a child pretending to cook in the dramatic play center may be interested in using a cookbook to help him prepare a feast for his friends. Parents rocking babies in the same center can use small board books to "read" to their offspring. A child in the block center may find inspiration for his structures in the picture books housed there.

MOTIVATING YOUR STUDENTS

Helping your students develop a love of reading and the motivation to do so in the preschool years is crucial in determining the trajectory of their future success as readers. But don't be surprised if you encounter a child every now and then who struggles to find their motivation and love of reading. Just remember: it's much easier to help young children develop a love of books and reading now than it is when they're nine years old.

One way to get young children excited about reading is to create class books using photos of each child's face. Often, the books that are the most popular in my classroom aren't the ones with the brightest characters on the front covers. Instead, they're books the children have helped create and incorporate photos of themselves and their classmates.

I created a book with my students by inviting the children to bring empty food boxes from home. The children were highly motivated to read this book because we created it using items that were meaningful to them. Then, I added predictable text to the pages that included each student's name and picture. The children chose to "read" this book over and over again because they felt

Figure 8.3

supported by the predictable and familiar text and were confident in their ability to "read" it. After reading a book like this aloud to your class, place it in your
classroom library where your students can enjoy reading it all year long.

The print that appears in the world around us in the form of traffic signs,
street signs, and business signs is often referred to as environmental print
(Neumann, Hood, & Ford, 2011). This also includes the logos on the boxes
and cans on the shelves in your cupboards and grocery stores. Simply calling
attention to this print in your classroom and throughout your school can go a
long way in motivating your students. Remember Hector from Chapter 7? He
was so motivated by environmental print, he gained confidence in himself and
believed he could read.

Figure 8.4

Figure 8.5

You can use environmental print in more intentional ways in your classroom. The child in Figure 8.5 is "reading" environmental print sentences in a pocket chart while practicing several different print awareness skills at the same time. She's pointing to the words on the chart and matching spoken words with print. She's using the picture cues on the chart to help her construct the meaning of the text. When she gets to the end of each line of print, she follows the return sweep and moves her finger down and over to the left to begin reading the next line. Of course, she has no idea she's learning all of these things; she is pretending to be a reader and enjoying herself.

Here's what Julie, a member of the Teaching Trailblazers, experienced in her own classroom after attending one of our in-depth, on-demand video trainings on the topic of early literacy.

> I implemented the pocket chart today with "I can read" statements. The students were so excited. I noticed the students in our book corner were reading the sentences between books. The students in our dramatic play center moved the table and chairs closer to the chart so they could play school, teaching their friends to read the sentences.

As you begin to embrace these changes in your classroom you may encounter those who don't fully understand the purpose behind what you're trying to accomplish by using environmental print. To be proactive on behalf of the adults who may be entering your classroom (administrators, parents, etc.), you may want to include a brief explanation about any environmental print you use in class books, charts, or on bulletin boards where you might display this print. A brief and simple statement such as, "We are learning that print is what we read" will go a long way in avoiding any adult questions or conflicts.

Incorporating these concepts into your daily classroom routine isn't time consuming or difficult. Here's what Leslie, a member of the Teaching Trailblazers, had to say about teaching concepts of print in her classroom after watching just one of our more than 70 on-demand video trainings.

> I used a lot of your concepts of print ideas in my classroom and really liked how easy it was to incorporate them into my daily read-alouds. My students had great success mastering many of the skills.

> If Leslie can do it, so can you!

BELIEVING THEY CAN READ

In the very beginning of the emergent literacy process, young children often believe that the story taking place in a book is told only by the pictures in the book. After listening to many stories being read aloud to them over time, they will eventually begin to understand that the printed words on the pages can also be used to tell the story (Snow, Burns, & Griffin, 1998). This is an important step in the emergent literacy process. Young children often believe they can read books that adults have frequently read to them, although they're just mimicking reading behaviors.

During the lesson at the beginning of this chapter, I was merely demonstrating how print works, but the real learning of print awareness takes place when the children take ownership of the story and begin to believe they can read. You may be wondering what it looks like to take ownership of a book in the classroom? Here are some examples to help you get started:

Reading the big book again: After I was finished reading the big book, I didn't put it away. I did put a regular sized copy in the library center, but I left the big book on the easel intentionally. During center time, I opened the book to one of the pages where the main character was scrubbing an animal. I also placed several smaller pointers in a basket under the easel. Then, I invited students to visit this area and read the book on their own using the pointers.

Sentences in pocket chart: I wrote the words "In went the…" on three different sentence strips and placed them in a pocket chart near the big book easel. I also placed three pictures at the bottom of the pocket chart: a pig, a duck, and a cow. I invited the children to place the pictures in the pocket chart and use the pointers from the basket to read the sentences.

The children were highly motivated to engage in these activities because they felt a sense of ownership of the story. The predictable text in this book offered a supportive structure that gave the students the confidence and motivation to engage in these powerful learning activities independently.

When it comes to teaching print awareness skills, you don't need to own every picture book ever published—or build an addition on your house like Kay. Just being intentional about the books you do choose to read aloud and about how you introduce them to your students will offer plenty of opportunities for teaching print awareness. Reading a class favorite aloud multiple times throughout the year will increase student engagement and motivation to read.

Figure 8.6

When children read, retell, or recite a familiar book, they are using cognitive skills that go way beyond simple memorization (Collins & Glover, 2015).

If you're wondering where to find these unicorn books young children love, or you just want somebody to hand you a list so you can order them from your local library, you can find more than 50 age-appropriate book lists for young children at Pre-K Pages: https://www.pre-kpages.com/category/book-lists/.

Chapter 9
Print Awareness Reflection

Remember the HEART method we discussed in Chapter 6, that gives you an opportunity to plan future lessons/activities and also reflect on the lesson you just taught? As it turns out, that's not a one-time thing. Let's explore how to align Step 2 (print awareness) with the HEART method and boost the effectiveness of your teaching.

Hands-on: When it comes to developing print awareness, you must provide your students with daily opportunities to hold books in their hands and interact with print throughout the classroom.

Enticing: Choose high-quality books that are both interesting and meaningful to your students. Even if you don't have access to a huge selection of books, just a handful of the *right* books will give your students plenty of exposure to concepts of print.

A connection: Begin introducing your students to a new "friend" (book) by inviting your students to make personal connections to the books by asking them questions. Remember the lesson in Chapter 8 when I asked the children if they had ever been to a farm? There's nothing young learners enjoy more than telling you about their own experiences!

Repeated exposure: Although you may feel an urge to constantly bring new titles into your classroom, don't be afraid to read the same book multiple times to teach different skills. Each time you read the same book you're deepening your students' connection to the book. For example, the lesson I described in Chapter 8 was the first time I read the book *Mrs. Wishy-Washy* aloud to my students, but we ended up reading it many more times throughout the year to teach different print and phonological awareness skills.

Time: Provide your students with a brief, but dedicated time each day to look at books. Because children thrive with structure and routine, this time each day will feel special—a lovely visit with new "friends" they can look forward to, and that will give them a feeling of security and comfort.

Although it's easy to remember to incorporate the HEART method to plan new activities and lessons for your students, it's also important to remember that your most valuable tool in growing as an effective teacher is reflection. Effective teachers develop a habit of reflection—what went well and what didn't—and then they continuously adjust their instruction to meet the needs of their students.

REFLECTION

As you begin to reflect on the information shared in Step 2, stop and think about what you're already doing that follows the HEART method. There's no need to completely change everything you're doing in your classroom. In fact, I'm willing to bet you're already doing some of these things outlined in Step 2. Pause for a moment and write down those things you're already doing. When you write your reflections on paper, they become more meaningful and help you see the progress you're making or have already made.

CHALLENGE

Next, I challenge you to identify just one thing you learned in Step 2 that you're not already doing in your classroom. Choose a new objective or practice that feels "doable" to you. If you choose something that's a big departure from the way you normally teach, you'll quickly become overwhelmed and discouraged. The most effective changes take place slowly, over time.

SELF-ASSESSMENT

After you have made that one small change in your classroom, stop and ask yourself the following questions:

How did it go?

How did it make me feel?

Is there anything I want to change or do differently next time?

TROUBLESHOOTING

If you're struggling to successfully establish a dedicated reading time each day, you're not alone. Here's what one of our Teaching Trailblazers members recently reported about her experience getting started with a regular, predictable reading time in her classroom:

My kids destroyed my books today—it was total chaos!

That quote brings to mind noise, arguing among the children, and a free-for-all environment that would make *me* want to hide in the closet (or at the very least, hit up my secret top-drawer stash of chocolate!). But just remember: it's normal to struggle with something the very first time you give it a try. Do you remember learning how to ride a bike or roller skate? It wasn't easy... but once you learned the basic principles and had plenty of time to practice, fail, make corrections, and then get up and practice again, it was much easier. Whenever you struggle with something in your teaching, it just means you need to reflect on what went well and adjust what didn't go well. A teacher who encounters a problem like kids destroying books needs to spend more time introducing books to children and more time modeling how to look at books appropriately.

Think of it like this: if you're running up against problems implementing a new procedure, it means you're trying to sell your students something they're not ready to buy. Before you can get their buy-in, you must create the *magic* around books and reading for them. You can do this by selecting only the best picture books that you know will hold the interest of your students. Then, you can demonstrate how much you love reading by saying the words out loud, daily and in front of them. Give it a try right now: stop and say it out loud along with me, "I love books! I love to read!" I would even take it a step further and add why you like that book—for example, "I learned so much about bugs when I read this book!" And finally, you must develop a habit of reading with enthusiasm and expression, no holds barred, no excuses. You know that quote "Dance like nobody's watching"? In this case, it's "Read like nobody's watching!"

Other factors to consider are your purpose and your actions during your dedicated reading time . If children are left unsupervised during this time it will backfire on you (if you've experienced a preschool version of *Lord of the Flies* like I have, you know what I'm talking about!). If you give too much time for the students to look at books and that time doesn't match their attention spans, things will get out of control quickly. Finally, if you're just using the books to fill time in your classroom, your students will sense this, and it will not be time well spent. When you believe in the value of a short, daily dedicated time for reading books and you're present to support your students throughout the process, then they'll ultimately be more successful.

Here's another objection I encounter often when it comes to dedicated reading time: "They fight over certain books." This is a good problem to have and an easy one to fix. First things first, if your kids are fighting over their favorite books, then you've succeeded in introducing the book well and your students feel a connection to the book—well done, you!

Most experts will tell you that if your students are fighting over a book it's a great opportunity to teach problem-solving skills. I don't disagree, but when it comes to books and reading, I don't think it's the best opportunity for teaching these skills. There are multiple times each day to teach problem-solving skills in any early childhood classroom. Remember Kay from Chapter 7 and her theory about introducing books to children? I challenge you to provide your students with multiple copies of the books they love the most. You don't have to go overboard like Kay and build an addition on your home; just a few copies will suffice.

I also strongly believe that there should be more books in your classroom library than there are children in the classroom. Making choices about which book to read is so important to your students, especially when you're trying to establish the love of reading and their motivation to read. Invite your students to make choices about which books they will read and provide them with more than one copy of the most popular books you know they will love. Every time you allow children the freedom to choose in your classroom, you're inviting them to take control of their own learning.

Imagine if you really wanted to read your favorite author's latest book, but your library had only 20 books total on the shelves. If you didn't get to the library first, that popular book would be long gone. Would you be excited about going to the library again tomorrow? Probably not. Now imagine if there was more than one copy of that book: your odds of getting that book would increase. Do you see where I'm going here?

Here's what another member of the Teaching Trailblazers had to say about incorporating daily time for reading in her classroom:

> This week we had a school assembly on Friday morning. My kids are so used to reading at a certain time that when I told them we had to skip it to go to the assembly they all groaned. That's when I knew all my hard work had really paid off!

By following the HEART method for exposing your students to concepts of print, and by engaging in continuous reflection after new lessons are taught, you'll ensure that you continue growing as a teacher...and your students will learn more, more easily. Don't forget, you have access to additional resources that support and extend the ideas in Step 2 at http://www.pre-kpages.com/TeachSmarter. There you can join our free "I Love Reading" challenge and connect with other early childhood professionals. You'll also discover how to create a quick and easy classroom library checkout system that even preschoolers can use independently. And don't miss my best tips for setting up a functional classroom library that your students will enjoy visiting as well as 12 engaging environmental print activities.

In Step 3 we'll be focusing on another critical ingredient in this recipe for prereading success—phonological awareness. We'll delve into what phonological awareness is, why it's important, and how young children learn this crucial skill.

STEP 3

Phonological Awareness

Chapter 10

Phonological Awareness: What It Is and Why It's Important

My grandmother was a wonderful baker. She picked her own blueberries and made the most amazing pies ever. Those sweet, juicy berries exploded in my mouth with each bite. Her rich, flaky crust was perfectly layered in a lattice pattern on top and sprinkled with sugar, just the way I liked it. As a child, my involvement in the baking process was limited to eating her delicious pies, but behind every good pie is a recipe that includes important instructions and ingredients.

Although my grandmother made delicious pies for more than fifty years, as she aged, her recipe began to slowly change. Once she was no longer able to pick blueberries herself, she started purchasing blueberries from the grocery store. Eventually she developed type 2 diabetes and cut back on the amount of sugar she put in her pies. I'm sorry to say that her once delicious pies were no longer delicious—in fact, they weren't very good at all. Of course, we continued to eat those pies with smiles on our faces, but my point is that when she was no longer able to follow the recipe, the pies were ruined. My grandmother's recipe for pie required certain ingredients and steps to follow. If my grandmother missed a step or left out certain ingredients, the pie just didn't taste as good as it normally did.

Much like my grandmother's recipe, teaching emergent literacy skills to young children requires certain steps. So far, in our recipe for prereading success, we've covered how young children learn the alphabet and also the importance of print awareness. Now, we're going to add another critical ingredient to our recipe for reading success: phonological awareness. Without this important ingredient, no matter how many other ingredients are present, young children will struggle to become successful readers later.

WHAT IS PHONOLOGICAL AWARENESS?

Phonological awareness refers to the ability to hear, identify, and manipulate the sounds in spoken language (Lonigan, Burgess, Anthony, & Barker, 1998). It's not the same as phonics, which involves knowing how written letters relate to spoken sounds. Activities that help young children develop phonological awareness skills provide practice with rhyme, beginning sounds, and syllables (Cassano & Rohde, 2019).

Before we begin to examine what phonological awareness is, it's important to note what it's *not*:

Phonological awareness is not phonics.

Phonological awareness does not involve words in print.

Phonological awareness is not a curriculum.

COMPONENTS OF PHONOLOGICAL AWARENESS

The term phonological awareness doesn't describe just one skill; it includes many different, yet equally important skills. This is what makes teaching phonological awareness skills tricky. Think of it like this: if you're following this recipe for reading success and one of the ingredients is listed as "spices," what do you do? Spices might mean different things to different people. How many spices? Which spices? Think of phonological awareness as the "spices" in this recipe. In order to add the correct amounts and types of spices, you need to know the name of each one and the role it plays in creating a successful outcome.

The ability to hear, identify, and manipulate the sounds in spoken language has been proven to help young children become better readers. Even before they learn to read and identify the letters of the alphabet, children can say the sounds they hear in spoken language. When they can hear the sounds in a word and identify where the sounds occur in the word, they are developing strong prereading skills (Cassano & Rohde, 2019).

The following are considered the critical components of phonological awareness:

Blending and Segmenting Phonemes

Phonemes are the smallest units of sound that distinguish between the meanings of words (Yopp & Yopp, 2000).

Initial sound isolation: What is the first sound in *mop*?

Final sound isolation: What is the last sound in *mop*?

Tells difference between single phonemes: Which one is different? /s/ /s/ /k/

Orally blends two or three phonemes into one word: What word am I trying to say? /m/ /o/ /p/

Onset-Rime Blending and Segmentation

Onset refers to the beginning sound, and rime refers to the letters that follow, usually a vowel and final consonants. Words that exemplify onset-rime are also commonly referred to as word families or CVC (consonant, vowel, consonant) words.

Orally blends onset-rimes: What word is this? /c/ at

Syllable Blending and Deletion

Identifies number of syllables in spoken words: claps syllables in one-, two-, and three-syllable words

Orally blends syllables: What word is this? "mon-key"

Sentence Segmentation

"I have a dog" = four different words

Alliteration

Words that have the same initial sound: Marvelous Monday, Terrific Tuesday, etc.

Rhyming

(Identifying rhyming words) Do *cat* and *mat* rhyme?

(Produces a rhyming word) Tell me a word that rhymes with nose?

Sound Word Discrimination

Tells whether words or sounds are the same or different: cat/cat (same) cat/car (different)

Identifies which word is different: sun, fun, sun (fun is different)

WHY ARE PHONOLOGICAL AWARENESS SKILLS IMPORTANT?

My former neighbor, Carla, was a nurse with two daughters, Priscilla and Caitlyn. I used to buy Girl Scout cookies from Caitlyn, and both girls came to our house to trick-or-treat each year. Carla and I were friendly, but we didn't socialize much beyond those annual exchanges. Her younger child, Priscilla, was a bubbly and energetic six-year-old who often asked if she could pet my dog whenever I passed by on my walks.

Then, one evening in early October, Carla showed up on my doorstep with a worried expression on her face. She knew I was a teacher and didn't waste any time getting to the point of her visit. She explained that Priscilla had recently started first grade, but things were not going well at all. Carla had been receiving daily phone calls from Priscilla's first-grade teacher complaining about her disruptive behavior. Priscilla was crying on the way to and from school each day and often woke up with a stomachache, begging her mother to allow her to stay home. How could this six-year-old child go from cheerful and bubbly to a behavior problem, seemingly overnight?

As I asked Carla a few questions about this mysterious behavior, I began to have my suspicions about what the issue was. According to her teacher, Priscilla wasn't doing her schoolwork, and she was often disruptive and disrespectful in class. Her teacher was also concerned about her grades and had already recommended that Priscilla receive tutoring after school. When it came time to do her homework, Carla reported that it was a nonstop battle that often ended with tears—from both mother and child. I quickly offered to meet with Priscilla on Saturday morning to see if we could get to the bottom of things.

On Saturday morning Carla and Priscilla both arrived on my doorstep at 10 a.m. sharp. Priscilla seemed to be her happy-go-lucky self and immediately started petting my dog. Carla gave me a copy of Priscilla's recent progress report from school, which painted a very bleak picture of Priscilla's academic progress in first grade thus far. I had brought a few items from my classroom home, and Priscilla and I sat down to investigate them together.

I started by reading aloud a fun rhyming story, then I asked Priscilla to match some small objects that rhymed, like a hat and a bat. We did a similar exercise with beginning sounds. By the end of our session, it was quite evident that Priscilla was missing one critical ingredient in the recipe for reading success. That missing ingredient that was causing her academic difficulties (as well as her stomachaches and behavior changes) was phonological awareness.

Priscilla couldn't sound out basic words because she couldn't identify pho-nemes (the sounds made by each letter). But it wasn't just phonemes; Priscilla lacked a basic understanding of almost every component of phonological awareness. Not only did she struggle to sound out basic words like *cat*, she also didn't understand onset-rime. This meant when she saw the word *hat*, she would have to sound out each letter again instead of just the initial sound. She spent so much time struggling to sound out words without fully understanding the sounds each one made that the meaning of what she did read was com-pletely lost to her.

In case you're wondering about Priscilla, everything turned out fine. I tutored her on Saturdays for the remainder of her first-grade year, and she eventually caught up to her peers. The behaviors and stomachaches disap-peared as she gained phonological awareness skills, and the confidence she needed to become a successful reader grew as well. But that's not the case for all children. Those who begin first grade without phoneme-level awareness may experience reading difficulties that persist throughout their elementary years (Juel & Leavell, 1988; Spira, Bracken, & Fischel, 2005).

Now that we know what phonological awareness is, in Chapter 11 we'll take a closer look at how young children acquire phonological awareness skills. By the time you've finished Chapter 11 you'll have a better understanding of where to begin and when to teach these skills to your students. After that, in Chapter 12 we'll look at different ways you can teach these skills that won't leave you feeling overwhelmed or frustrated.

Chapter 11
Where to Start with Phonological Awareness

In Chapter 10 we covered the basic components of phonological awareness. In this chapter we're going to look more closely at how these skills develop and when to start teaching them. Remember my grandmother's recipe for blueberry pie? Her recipe required specific ingredients and steps to follow. If she skipped steps or eliminated certain ingredients, the outcome wasn't as good as it should be. But baking the perfect pie isn't just about adding the correct ingredients; the timing for adding the ingredients and the order they're added can also play a big part in achieving the desired results. If the individual components of phonological awareness skills are the spices in this so-called recipe for reading success, then we need to consider the correct amounts of each skill and when to add—or teach them—to achieve the desired results.

The research around phonological awareness has gained more attention over the past two decades. One of the most exciting discoveries is that phonological awareness can be developed through carefully planned instruction, which has a significant influence on reading and spelling achievement (Ball & Blachman, 1991; Bryant, MacLean, Bradley, & Crossland, 1990; Byrne & Fielding-Barnsley, 1989, 1991; O'Connor, Jenkins, Leicester, & Slocum, 1993). Although the research is there, the differences between phonological awareness, phonemic awareness, and phonics can be difficult to understand, convey, and execute.

I once worked with the leaders of an early childhood campus who had mandated 10-minute blocks of time each day devoted to whole-group phonological awareness instruction. You see, they had received the test scores from the first nine weeks of school and deemed them unacceptable. They wanted teachers to improve their phonological awareness instruction to raise the students' assessment scores. Each component of phonological awareness was plugged into a handy five-day plan that made perfect sense...*to the adults who created it.* But as you know, the simplest plan on paper doesn't necessarily translate to the students' practical learning.

The plan teachers were given required them to teach only one phonological awareness skill each day during a designated, school-wide time period from 9:00–9:10 a.m. Mondays were for rhyming, Tuesdays were for alliteration, Wednesdays were for sentence segmentation, Thursdays were for syllables, and Fridays were for onset-rime. When students in a class had mastered one skill, teachers were instructed to replace that day with phoneme instruction. The method of instruction was left up to the teachers, which resulted in confusion over what these lessons should look like. Although everything appeared to be nice and tidy on paper, this approach was completely contrary to how phonological awareness skills are actually learned.

Because you've already discovered that learning the alphabet isn't a linear process that starts with A and ends with Z, it won't come as any surprise to you that learning phonological awareness skills isn't linear, either. By focusing on only one skill each day in our classrooms, this plan removed these fundamental skills from their natural context. This rigid approach to phonological awareness didn't take into consideration that some children weren't ready for sentence segmentation—so what, for example, would they do on Wednesdays? This rigid instruction would be completely lost on them, wasting their precious time (and ours as teachers!).

When you teach certain components of phonological awareness before young children are ready for them, you'll be stuck rolling that heavy boulder uphill once again. Each child acquires phonological awareness skills at their own pace. Often, the speed at which they acquire these skills is related to their individual experiences and prior exposure to language at home. Although some children may have acquired certain components of phonological awareness before entering your classroom, others will need intentional guidance and support from you while under your care to help them develop these skills.

Teaching early literacy skills like phonological awareness would be so much easier if all young children developed these critical skills at the same pace. Unfortunately, that's not how the emergent literacy process works. But although there isn't a one-size-fits-all formula that you can follow that will magically teach your students all the different components of phonological awareness at the right time, there *are* some ways you can make it easier for your students to acquire these crucial skills. If you're feeling overwhelmed, don't worry because I'm going to walk you through it step by step and you'll feel so much better by the end of Step 3. Let's look at the following chart.

Don't let this chart fool you: although it shows the different components of phonological awareness and the general sequence in which some young children may learn these skills, the process is neither linear nor sequential. For example, children can be learning more than one of these skills at a time. Although syllable awareness is evident before onset-rime and onset-rime before phonemes, demonstration of more complex levels of phonological awareness is evident even as children are mastering lesser ones (Anthony, Lonigan, Driscoll, Phillips, & Burgess, 2003).

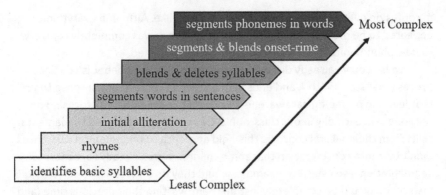

Figure 11.1

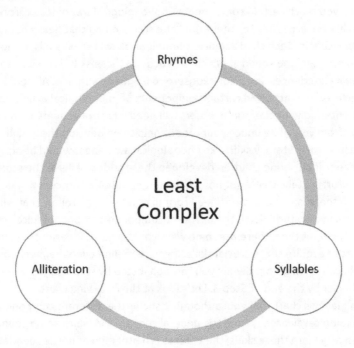

Figure 11.2

Let's take a closer look at some of the least complex skills. These skills are not dependent upon one another; therefore, it's not necessary to introduce them in a rigid sequence. Young children can acquire rhyming awareness, alliteration, and basic syllables, all at the same time.

If you're wondering what it looks like to teach more than one skill at the same time, here's an example from my own classroom.

PAJAMAS AND LLAMAS

Any early childhood teacher who's been on the job for more than a few days knows how difficult it can be to capture the attention of young children, especially in the beginning of the school year. You're trying to establish your classroom routines and procedures while trying to teach academic content and address the social and emotional needs of your students—all at the same time. The very idea of trying to teach anything among the noise and chaos that is taking place in your classroom can seem like an impossible task.

Much of the chaos and noise in your classroom is due to the fact that young children have short attention spans. During the first few weeks of the school year, it's difficult to see the forest for the trees. You have so much to teach, and it seems like you'll never be able to get to it all by the end of the year! But what if instead of blocking out your schedule by the major concepts you plan to teach, you broke down everything you had to teach right now into bite-sized chunks that matched the attention spans of your students? Slow and steady wins the race.

One year, my class wasn't as engaged as I would have liked them to be during read-aloud time. I pulled out one of my go-to books, *Llama Llama Red Pajama* (Dewdney, 2005) to see if it would help capture their attention and also help me introduce my students to a few important early literacy skills at the same time. I like to compare this approach to hiding veggies in their macaroni and cheese. You know your students need a well-balanced diet of early literacy skills, yet teaching them these skills (especially in the beginning of the school year) can be a challenge for even the most seasoned veteran teacher.

We gathered on the rug for our morning read-aloud time. I pulled the book out from under my chair where I kept my books and props for each day. As I expected, a few children said they were already familiar with this story. I had my pat response ready. "Yes, but you've never heard *me* read it before," I said. Together, we looked at the cover of the book and discussed what we noticed in the picture. I explained what pajamas were (just in case my dual language learners were unfamiliar with the word or its meaning) and asked the students if they had clothes they liked to sleep in. This elicited a chorus of excited responses eager to share about their own pajamas in a wide variety of colors and covered with popular characters.

Next, I pointed out the title as well as the names of the author and illustrator. Because I was aiming for increased engagement, I added, "This is one of my very favorite books of all time! I like the way the words sound when I say them. If you listen closely, maybe you'll hear them too." As I read the book aloud with great enthusiasm and expression, I emphasized the rhyming words at the end of each sentence and invited the children to chime in with me. Of course, it was still early in the year and only a few of the children caught on to this nuance, but those who did were even more motivated to listen to and participate in the reading of the story.

Because it was early in the year, I didn't stop reading the book to focus on any other phonological awareness skills besides rhyming. Instead, I asked a few questions afterwards to call attention to another component of phonological awareness: syllables. "I like how the words 'mama' and 'llama' sounded in the story. Can you say them with me?" I asked. After we said the words "mama llama" aloud together I continued, "Did you hear how the words sounded the same at the end?" I repeated the words aloud, emphasizing the final syllable. "Now let's try clapping each word, like this," I demonstrated clapping twice, once for each syllable in the word *mama* and then again for the word *llama*. Then I invited the children to join me in clapping the syllables. This entire process after I had finished reading the book took approximately two minutes.

I hope this personal story has allowed you to see the light at the end of the phonological awareness tunnel. By reading through one single book, I was able to bring in rhyming awareness and basic syllables—at the same time. Although the concept of phonological awareness can be difficult to fully grasp at first, it is quite easy to teach once you have the training and support you need to do it well. In Chapter 12 we'll look more closely at some practical ideas to help you get started teaching phonological awareness skills to the students in your own classrooms.

Chapter 12

Your Phonological Awareness Questions Answered

W hat makes teaching phonological awareness skills so tricky is that they're not concrete, there's nothing to see or touch, it's all auditory. In addition, there are many different components of phonological awareness to teach—and young children learn them at their own pace. Then there's the problem of teaching these skills in a way that is meaningful, fun, and engaging for your students. It can seem impossible at times, and it often takes good teachers years to develop, define, and perfect their techniques. Here are some of the most frequently asked questions teachers have when it comes to teaching phonological awareness skills in the classroom.

HOW DO I KNOW WHICH PHONOLOGICAL AWARENESS SKILLS MY STUDENTS KNOW?

Let's think back to Chapter 4 where we discussed how to determine which letters your students know. Assessment is a data collection process used to inform your instruction as a professional educator. The way you find out what your students know about any skill or subject is to conduct assessment. But just because you're assessing a certain skill doesn't mean you should expect full mastery of that skill each time it's assessed. Until we can begin to understand the true purpose of assessment, it will continue to seem irrelevant. The objective of assessment isn't just to find out what your students don't know—it's about becoming aware of both what they know now and what they need to learn next.

Assessment can often be misunderstood by administrators as well. Most public pre-K programs receive funding from the federal government and states. This means that the entity providing the funding will require proof of learning to ensure their money is being well spent. This proof is usually delivered in the form of assessment data. The problem with this model is that often the administrators who deliver the data collected, or the entity receiving the data, don't fully understand its true purpose.

Remember my grandmother's delicious blueberry pie recipe? If you think of assessment as proof that the recipe was properly followed (i.e., the student can read!), then the data will never look good enough until it's perfect. If the data are viewed as understanding *exactly where* a student's literacy growth process is in the "recipe," however—so you know what students need to learn next—then assessment will become helpful to teachers, parents, and ultimately students, instead of feeling punitive.

As with letter knowledge, after you've conducted your assessments and analyzed your data of phonological awareness, you can determine where each of your students is in their individual stages of phonological awareness development. Then, you can begin to determine your plan of action when it comes to adding in opportunities to develop these specific skills throughout your day. Don't get discouraged if your students aren't consistently demonstrating their knowledge of certain phonological awareness skills that you've taught and thought they learned. Typically, children younger than four years old do not demonstrate phonological awareness reliably (Lonigan, Burgess, & Anthony, 2000). One day they may appear to "get" a phonological awareness concept, and the very next day, they may appear to have lost it! If you're teaching young children, this is perfectly normal.

WHEN SHOULD I START TEACHING LETTER SOUNDS?

In the beginning of my teaching career I taught letters and sounds from the very beginning of the school year, but not together. What I didn't realize was that I could combine teaching letters and sounds together for a more seamless learning experience. Eventually, as I attended more professional development sessions and gained more classroom experience, I learned how to pair teaching of the letter names with their sounds.

I'll never forget the year I tried this method for the first time. I started out teaching the letters in context from the first day of school like I always did, but I added letter sounds as well as songs and movements to go along with each letter. The result? It was like somebody had flipped the light switch on in my classroom. My students responded to this method so well that by late October, many of them had learned all their letters and sounds. But if you had asked them, they would have told you that they played all day and had fun at school. I'd call that a win in my book!

There are a few different ways to combine letter learning with letter sounds. The methods I've had the most success with incorporate a multisensory approach. A multisensory approach includes seeing, saying, hearing, and moving to teach a concept (Baker & Jordan, 2015; Jordan & Baker, 2011). This is often accomplished by using fun, catchy songs that also incorporate hand motions, movements, or sign language. But don't just take my word for it; Here's what researchers had to say about teaching letters and sounds at the same time: Combining phoneme level instruction with alphabet knowledge is both effective and efficient in helping children understand the associations between phonemes and graphemes—the written representation of auditory sounds (Sénéchal, Ouellette, Pagan, & Lever, 2012).

WHAT IF I DON'T HAVE ENOUGH TIME IN MY DAY TO TEACH PHONOLOGICAL AWARENESS SKILLS?

I taught half-day public prekindergarten for 10 years. During those 10 years my colleagues and I complained daily about how there was never enough time to teach everything that was required of us. Throughout this 10-year period, my colleagues and I took every opportunity we could to lobby for full-day pre-K at the district level. There were school districts out there making it work, so why couldn't we?

We mistakenly thought that full-day prekindergarten would solve all of our problems because we would finally have all the time we needed to "fit it all in." By 2008 we had all but given up hope that we would ever move to full-day classes, and then it suddenly happened. Being the squeakiest wheel had finally paid off. We floated back to school in the fall of 2009, prepped for full-day pre-K and filled with anticipation of having our best year ever. But instead of finally being able to "fit it all in" we found ourselves right back at square one, struggling to find the time to teach everything that was required. By the time we were finished with breakfast, it was time for lunch, then a nap, and some days we felt like we had less time than ever before.

The moral of this story is that there will *never* be enough time in any day to teach all that needs to be taught. The great thing about phonological awareness skills, though, is that they can be woven naturally into what you're already doing in your classroom. Do you sing songs with your students daily? Songs help develop important rhyming skills in a supportive and playful way. Reading books with rhyming text is another natural way to add phonological awareness skills daily.

WHY CAN'T MY STUDENTS RHYME? I READ RHYMING BOOKS ALL THE TIME AND WE SING SONGS DAILY—AM I MISSING SOMETHING?

This is a great question, and one I receive often. Although phonological awareness encompasses many different skills, some of the more complex skills can be broken down even further. I know—confusing, right? When it comes to breaking down a phonological awareness skill, it's important to know that they typically follow a sequence:

Fill in the blank: "Cat in the..."

Identifies the same: Using yes or no answers. "I'm going to say two words, you tell me if they rhyme. Cat, hat, do these words rhyme?"

Generates: "What rhymes with cat?"

Children demonstrate phonological awareness through three task categories that vary in complexity: detection (identifying similar sounds), synthesis (blending smaller linguistic units into syllables or words), and analysis (manipulating linguistic units or producing examples).

1. Detection
2. Synthesis
3. Analysis

(Cassano & Schickedanz, 2015; Stanovich, Cunningham, & Cramer, 1984; Yopp, 1988)

I TEACH INFANTS; SHOULD I BE TEACHING RHYMING SKILLS?

That's the beauty of rhyming skills: it doesn't matter if you teach infants, toddlers, preschoolers, pre-K, or kindergarten. You can teach rhyming skills to all these age groups because rhyming is an auditory skill that is best taught through reading books and singing songs.

ARE NONSENSE WORDS OKAY FOR RHYMING?

Yes, absolutely! Rhyming is all about playing with language and manipulating sounds. Nonsense words are completely appropriate.

HOW CAN I TEACH RHYMING TO MY STUDENTS WHOSE FIRST LANGUAGE ISN'T ENGLISH?

When working with dual language learners it's important that you have three-dimensional objects your students can touch and feel when you start teaching rhyming skills. Flat pictures of objects won't be as effective.

If you need additional help planning activities that support phonological awareness, don't worry! That's what the next chapter is all about.

Chapter 13

What Learning Phonological Awareness Skills Looks Like

How quickly children begin to grasp phonological awareness skills is often related to the length of time they've been exposed to phonological processes. For example, if you work with children who have limited language experiences or for whom opportunities to learn these concepts at home have been sparse, they may need more time and exposure to certain phonological awareness skills before they will begin to develop them. Therefore, it's imperative that we sprinkle opportunities for developing phonological awareness skills throughout every school day, all year long. You may also notice that those students who come from homes where they have been read aloud to often have better phonological awareness skills—that's simply because these skills are closely tied to language development.

Now that you know what phonological awareness is, what the different components are, and when to teach them, let's explore some practical ways you can teach these skills to young children. We already know that phonological awareness is all about the sounds we hear in language, so it only makes sense that worksheets and workbooks aren't practical when it comes to teaching or learning these skills. Following you'll find a list of highly effective methods you can use to support the development of phonological awareness skills.

Songs

Nursery rhymes

Poems

Hands-on activities

SINGING WITHOUT WALLS

I once taught in Houston on a campus with no walls. I'm sure there was a reason the school was designed this way, but it made teaching pre-K extremely difficult. I didn't fully grasp the severity of the situation until a few days before school began. I was preparing my daily picture schedule and humming one of my favorite preschool songs quietly to myself. Then it suddenly dawned on me: the lack of walls meant that I may not be able to sing songs with my students as often as I normally would. What if the teacher next to me was trying to conduct a whole-group lesson while we were singing?

I felt sick to my stomach as I took stock of how often I sang with my students each day. We sang a good morning song, transition songs, circle time songs, and a good-bye song. In total, I counted a total of six songs that we sang in our classroom daily, and that didn't include songs to go along with specific lessons and themes. At that moment, I seriously doubted my ability to teach well without using songs and music each day.

You see, songs aren't just fun; they can be used to teach many academic skills to your students as well. Everything from math to phonological awareness, oral language, and more can be learned through songs and music. All children can benefit from the daily use of songs and music in the classroom. Dual language learners and students with special needs thrive with the supportive structure songs and music have to offer, as well as their repetitive nature and rhythm. Songs expose children to rhyming, repetition, and the rhythm of language, which helps them eventually read fluently with expression and animation in their voice.

Most important, songs and music allow teachers to differentiate their instruction because each student gets exactly what they need from participating in songs and music. Some children may be gaining rhyming skills, while others are developing oral language and vocabulary skills. And kinesthetic learners can gain the same skills in a way that best meets their learning style if actions and motions are put to the tune of the music. Even quiet and shy students who don't seem to be getting anything from music are still benefiting as they listen and internalize the rhythms and rhymes, although it may not be visible to us as adults.

My colleagues gently coaxed me off the ledge and explained that we had a dedicated music time at 10:45 a.m. each day while the kindergarten classes next to us went to the playground. Although this was far from ideal, I did make it through that school year—and promptly moved on to a classroom with four walls where I could sing with my students all day long.

NURSERY RHYMES

I'm an unapologetic proponent of nursery rhymes because I've seen how powerful they can be when it comes to helping young children develop phonological awareness skills. But I didn't fully understand the true power of nursery rhymes until our state released a new set of early childhood standards. My colleagues and I were racking our brains trying to figure out how we were going to fit all the new emergent literacy standards into our already jam-packed school days. We tossed around idea and after idea, each one more complex than the last. Finally, we decided we didn't need to reinvent the wheel entirely. Instead, we could use what we'd already been doing and just be more intentional about how we taught these skills.

We'd already been using nursery rhymes with great success in our program for several years and we'd witnessed firsthand how our students had flourished with each new rhyme we introduced. They bonded with the rhymes and eagerly anticipated the next one to be revealed. They felt confident when "reading" these rhymes, which led to motivation to read. And so, the question arose: What if we started to focus on certain aspects of phonological awareness at the same time we were learning each rhyme? We weren't entirely sure this plan would work, but it seemed like the most natural way to teach phonological awareness skills, so we gave it a try.

It wasn't long before we began to notice how easily our students were learning these new skills. They were filling in the rhyming words at the end of the lines in each poem, and they were clapping the syllables in words like Humpty and Dumpty. Because the poems were short, they were perfect for counting words in a sentence. Our plan hadn't just worked; it had naturally helped our students skyrocket their phonological awareness skills right away.

POEMS

Years later, one of my jobs as an instructional specialist was to go into classrooms and conduct demonstration lessons for pre-K teachers. One day in mid-September I arrived in the classroom of a young teacher we'll call Charlotte. She was eager to have support and greeted me enthusiastically at the classroom door. I spent some time getting to know her students before starting my demo lesson. When it was finally time for my lesson to begin, I opened my gigantic teacher bag and pulled out a book and two red paper apples glued to craft sticks.

The lesson was going well until I finished the read-aloud portion and introduced the apples to the students. The apples were props to go along with the poem "Two Red Apples." At this point, Charlotte began to look nervous. She glanced toward the classroom door several times and squirmed in her seat. As I began to recite the poem with the children using the props, Charlotte bolted out of her chair and sprang toward the classroom door, closing it softly. I was curious, but I knew we had a debriefing session scheduled after class, so I made a mental note to ask her about her behavior later.

After the children had left for the day, Charlotte and I sat down at a small table. I didn't have to bring up the apple incident because Charlotte began to immediately apologize profusely. It turns out her principal had conducted a formal observation in her classroom the week before. During his debriefing session, the principal had made it very clear to Charlotte that he "wasn't paying her to play games all day long" and he expected to see her teaching the next time he visited her room.

Of course, I was devastated to learn that a school administrator didn't understand the rich learning that occurred when poems were used daily in the early childhood classroom. Confrontations with principals rarely end well, so instead, Charlotte and I crafted an extremely detailed lesson plan that laid out the exact standards Charlotte was covering in every single poem and song she planned to use in her classroom the following week. When the principal saw the enormous number of standards addressed in these detailed plans, he decided that Charlotte could continue singing and reciting poems with her students. *Whew!*

HANDS-ON ACTIVITIES

You're helping your students develop phonological awareness skills, now, at the early childhood level, so they can reach into their imaginary toolboxes and pull out the right tools for the right job at the right time. It's extremely difficult for children to learn how to read during the same fragile time they're still developing their phonological awareness skills. It can be overwhelming and confusing, and they will start to struggle—or worst-case scenario, they'll come to hate reading because they're so frustrated. But the good news is that we can help our kids become rhyming rock stars with fun, developmentally appropriate, easy, hands-on games, and activities.

During my time spent as an instructional specialist, I often met with small groups of students for literacy lessons. Once, using assessment data collected by the teacher, I gathered a small group of five children together on the rug in a pre-K classroom. Their teacher had been using student names to develop phonological awareness skills throughout the year. Based on the assessment data she had collected, she had determined that this group was ready for more targeted syllable instruction.

As the children plopped down on the rug in a semicircle facing me, their wide eyes were glued to the paper bag I had placed in front of me. "What's in there?" asked Justin, pointing to the bag inquisitively.

"Are they cookies? When we went to the pumpkin patch, we had cookies in a bag like that!" exclaimed Henry with a hopeful look in his eyes.

"No, they're not cookies, but I think you'll like what I have in here anyway." I replied slyly as I opened the bag and reached down inside. As I removed six small objects out of the bag, one by one, I asked the children to name them as I placed them on the floor in front of me. There was a wagon, a dog, a straw hat, an apple, a banana, and a small plastic rainbow.

I picked up the apple and held it up for the children to see, then invited them to pass it around so they could each have a turn holding it. As they took turns, I explained that some words have different parts that we can hear when we say their names out loud. "Some words have just one part, some have two parts, and some have three or even more parts," I explained further.

"The apple only has one part," said Clarissa, pointing to the apple.

"That's right, we can only see one part with our eyes, but if we close our eyes and listen to the word apple with our ears, we can hear two parts of the word," I said as I demonstrated by slowly saying the word app-le with my eyes closed. A few of the children mimicked me by closing their eyes and saying the word *apple* aloud.

"Let's try it another way," I said. I put the little plastic apple down on the carpet and clapped twice as I said the word *apple*, exaggerating the two different parts and clapping once as I said each syllable. Justin and Clarissa jumped right in and clapped twice along with me. Now it was time to extend the invitation to all the children to participate along with me. "Let's try it together, get your hands ready." We clapped twice while saying the word *apple*—so far so good!

Next, I gathered up all the items and put them back in the bag. Justin, thinking our game was over, started to get up and leave. "The game is just beginning, Justin. Now you get to pick something from the bag," I said. Justin quickly sat back down and tried to peer into the bag. I explained how I was going to pass the bag around and invite each child to close their eyes, reach into the bag, and select one item. Although closing their eyes for this game wasn't necessary, it added an element of mystery and fun that helped hold their attention and increase engagement.

After each child had selected an item from the bag, I invited them to take turns showing and telling the others about their item. "I got a wagon!" said Henry excitedly. Next, I invited one child at a time to hold up their object as we all clapped the syllables together. As Henry held up his prized wagon, I reminded the children to listen for the parts in the word as I said it aloud, then I asked them how many parts they heard in the word wagon. I counted the parts of the word on my fingers and clapped accordingly, and finally we all clapped the parts of the word together. "Henry, how many parts did you hear in the word *wagon*?" I asked. "I dunno," Henry said as he shrugged and raced his wagon across the carpet in front of him. Clarissa, Justin, and the other two students all shouted excitedly, "Two! There were two parts!"

I knew Henry's teacher had been using student names all year to teach phonological awareness skills, so I tried a different approach, "Henry, how many parts do you have in your name?" He stopped racing his wagon, thought about it for a moment and said, "One! I have one part!"

"Let's try it together," I invited. I closed my eyes and said his name out loud while emphasizing the two distinct parts. "Can you help me?" I asked. Henry and the other children in the small group clapped the two syllables in his name together. "Oh, yeah, I have two parts," he said as he continued to play with the wagon.

"Let's try listening to the parts in *wagon* again," I suggested. We tried it again and this time Henry participated and made the connection between the two parts he heard in the word *wagon* and the two parts in his name. This small-group lesson took 10 minutes from start to finish and was hands-on, fun, and engaging.

While the other four children in this group were easily grasping the concept of syllables, Henry wasn't quite there yet and needed a bit of extra support, and that's okay. We can't expect all children to learn phonological awareness skills at the same time; we must meet them wherever they are in their current stages of development and support them in their journey. Henry may need more time and exposure to syllables before he can fully grasp the concept. Although Henry had started out the year with his peers and he had learned alongside them, he was learning at his own individual pace.

One member of the Teaching Trailblazers, AnneMarie, was a seasoned pre-K classroom teacher. But once she was exposed to new, exciting ways to develop her students' phonemic awareness skills, things finally clicked into place for her. AnneMarie says,

I've been a Preschool Special Education Teacher for 27 years. When I joined the Teaching Trailblazers, I was amazed at what I didn't know about teaching preschool. I never learned why phonemic awareness was important, or the typical progression of developmental skills. I always taught as a special educator, but now I'm a preschool teacher with a special education background. Since becoming a member, I have seen my student's abilities go up and things I would never have tried before—like rhyming words, I am now seeing my students achieve.

With just a few subtle changes to the way you're already teaching, you'll revolutionize your teaching and your students' learning. When you have the ingredients you need, and you know when to add them to your emergent literacy recipe, the end results will be amazing. In terms of phonological awareness skills, those ingredients are songs, nursery rhymes, poems, and hands-on activities. In Chapter 14 you'll align what you've learned in Step 3 with the HEART method to set both you and your students up for success.

Chapter 14
Phonological Awareness Reflection

So far, you've applied the HEART method to Steps 1 and 2. Now it's time to align Step 3 (phonological awareness) with the HEART method to help your students develop the crucial skills they'll need to become successful readers. You can't skip Step 3 in this recipe for reading success. Remember that delicious blueberry pie? Phonological awareness is an important ingredient that, when left out, can leave your pie tasting bitter and—let's face it—inedible.

Before we begin, let's review the HEART method:

Hands-on

Enticing

A connection

Repeated exposure

Time for practice daily

Hands-on: This is perhaps the trickiest aspect of teaching phonological awareness because it's an auditory skill. Exactly how can you use hands-on methods to teach an auditory skill? Well, the key is to use three-dimensional objects whenever possible so your students have opportunities to touch, feel, and manipulate them.

Think of it like this: you can show your students a picture of an apple and ask them to clap the syllables, but then they'll only be able to see the apple with their eyes. Or, you can use the apple from your dramatic play center—or even a real apple—which will allow your students to touch and feel the apple. When you use three-dimensional objects in your lessons, you're engaging not only your students' sense of sight, but also their sense of touch. If you increase the number of senses engaged, you also increase student learning. Remember the bag of items I brought with me to the lesson I taught my students about syllables? Well, this fits perfectly with my motto: Flat is boring and 3-D is fun.

Enticing: Phonological awareness skills by themselves aren't naturally enticing skills to teach. It's entirely up to the teacher to use playful, fun, and natural opportunities to carefully entice and engage young children in learning these skills. Using songs, rhymes, and poems will go a long way in enticing your students to learn phonological awareness skills—and they won't even realize they're learning.

A connection: When you provide daily opportunities to sing songs, read nursery rhymes, and recite poems daily, your students will begin to develop a deep connection to them. In essence, these stories, nursery rhymes, and poems become part of the children's own experiences and identity.

When I worked on an elementary campus, the fifth graders would tour the school on graduation day to say good-bye to their previous teachers. Being a pre-K teacher, I understood that not all students would remember me because they were so young when they were in my class. When graduating fifth graders came to my classroom, they would often share fond memories of playing in certain centers or special events like field trips.

One year in particular, a young girl entered my classroom door on the last day of school to ask me to sign her yearbook. As she wandered around the classroom, she commented on a few of the physical things in the room that she remembered. Then, as she passed a display of stuffed nursery rhyme characters prominently displayed in a rain gutter, she suddenly spun around, eyes wide, and asked excitedly, "Do you still do Humpty Dumpty?"

I could tell from the expression on her face and the tone of her voice that the nursery rhyme Humpty Dumpty had clearly struck a happy chord with her. I replied, "I do, would you like to say it with me?" It didn't matter that she was in the fifth grade; she enthusiastically began to recite the rhyme along with me, including the movements I used each year to engage my students in the rhyme. Afterwards, she handed me her yearbook to sign and asked, "Can you write 'Humpty Dumpty' under your name, so I won't forget you?" she asked. I happily obliged.

Repeated exposure: When it comes to phonological awareness skills, repeated exposure is where it gets a little confusing. We know there are several different components of phonological awareness skills. And we also know that children don't learn these skills in a lockstep sequence, one after the other. We must be careful to not move on too quickly when we think our students have mastered it. Instead, we need to be mindful of how young children learn and continue to provide them with opportunities to practice all components of phonological awareness skills throughout the year. That doesn't mean you need to be doing small-group instruction for syllables if all of your students have demonstrated a basic understanding of this skill. Instead, it means that you should continue to sing songs, read nursery rhymes, recite poems, and provide hands-on opportunities in your classroom all year long. Recall your own experience raising your children, if that applies: Children can hear the same story over and over again (*Goodnight Moon*, I'm looking at you...) and still experience joy and wonder each time they hear it again. The same applies for the nursery rhymes, songs, and poems you bring to the classroom: Once is *never* enough, and planning a quick review of poems/songs/nursery rhymes previously learned, throughout the year, will help your students become fluent with phonological awareness.

Time: This is perhaps the easiest aspect of teaching phonological awareness skills. You can sing songs, read nursery rhymes, recite poems, and provide hands-on opportunities throughout the day, every day. When you understand the importance of these activities, then it should be easy to accomplish this portion of HEART.

We've already addressed the importance of reflection in Steps 1 and 2 and the critical role they play in your growth as an effective teacher. Effective teachers must develop a consistent habit of reflection to continuously adjust their instruction to meet the needs of their students.

REFLECTION

As you begin to reflect on the information shared in Step 3, take time to stop and think about what you're already doing that follows the HEART method. There's no need to completely change everything you're doing in your class-room. In fact, I'm willing to bet you're already doing some of these things out-lined in Step 3 on phonological awareness. Pause for a moment and write down those things you're already doing. When you write your reflections on paper, they become more meaningful and allow you to see the progress you're making or have already made more clearly.

CHALLENGE

Next, I challenge you to identify just one thing you learned in Step 3 that you're not already doing in your classroom. Choose a new objective or practice that feels "doable" to you. If you choose something that's a big departure from the way you normally teach, you'll quickly become overwhelmed and discouraged. The most effective changes take place slowly, over time.

SELF-ASSESSMENT

After you have made that one small change in your classroom, stop and ask yourself the following questions:

How did it go?

How did it make me feel?

Is there anything I want to change or do differently next time?

TROUBLESHOOTING

If you're encountering difficulty teaching a specific component of phonological awareness to your students, you're not alone. Here's what one of our Teaching Trailblazers members recently reported about her experience getting started with basic syllables in her classroom:

> I tried clapping the syllables in my students' names for the first time with them today and they just stared at me blankly. What am I doing wrong?

It's important to remember that the first time you do anything in your classroom is an initial exposure. However, mastery of a skill *never* comes after a single exposure. For example, when I was learning how to ride a bike, my father demonstrated it for me by riding his own bike around the driveway and up and down the street. Then, he helped me get on my own bike and try it out while he supported my bike. He didn't expect mastery after that first exposure, because he knew it would take me time and practice to learn the new skill. As wise, practical teachers, we can bring the same gentle expectations to our classrooms, knowing that "practice makes perfect," and for some, the practice period is longer than for others. But with practice, eventually your students will all master phonemic awareness skills.

Another thing to consider when planning activities that support phonemic awareness is the length of your initial exposure to the concept—in this case, syllables. If you have a large class of 15 or more students and you clap the syllables in each child's name to introduce the concept, you'll lose them by the time you get to the name of the third child (...and as for names 4–15? Forget about it!). Being an early childhood teacher is a constant balancing act: you have to take into consideration how young children learn, their attention spans, the content you have to teach, and the methods by which you teach that content. Don't beat yourself up if your initial lesson resulted in blank stares. Instead, take time to reflect on why it didn't work and what you can do differently next time. Slow and steady wins the race.

In the example of teaching syllables via the students' names, I would start by clapping a word from your read-aloud first. Then make the connection to the word in the book to your students' names. Then clap just two or three students' names to illustrate your point. Afterwards, reflect on how well these adjustments worked and go from there. You can always follow up that lesson with *another* example of syllable demonstration using words from the same read-aloud selection and then add two to three *more* children's names. It may seem like a long, drawn-out lesson, but in reality it will take you less than a week!

By following the HEART method for exposing your students to phonological awareness skills, and by engaging in continuous reflection after each new lesson is taught, you'll continue to hone your skills as a teacher...and your students will continue to learn.

If you would like additional support incorporating phonological awareness skills into your classroom, go to http://www.pre-kpages.com/TeachSmarter. There you'll find more information about phonological awareness, and the most effective hands-on phonological awareness activities your students will enjoy. You're also invited to join our free Phonological Awareness Challenge where you can network with other like-minded early childhood professionals who will lift you up and cheer you on every step of the way.

In Step 4 you'll learn the important role oral language plays in the emergent literacy process. Although oral language may seem like an overly simplistic skill to teach explicitly, it is in fact a very crucial ingredient in the recipe for reading success.

STEP 4

Oral Language

Chapter 15
Oral Language: What It Is and Why It's Important

Oral language is the system through which we use spoken words to express knowledge, ideas, and feelings (Lesaux & Harris, 2015). In much the same way young children learn to walk, learning to talk also develops over time and requires much practice. If taken solely at face value, oral language may seem like an overly simplistic term that's just a fancy way for educators to describe the ability to talk. But when you scratch beneath the surface, you'll discover that having strong oral language skills will help your students thrive—not just now, but for the rest of their lives. Oral language is the basis for human communication and social interaction (Wells, 1986).

So, what role does oral language play in the emergent literacy process? How can speaking and communicating help young children become better readers? You see, reading comprehension depends on language abilities that young children have been developing since birth (Kintsch, 2005). These language abilities also include basic vocabulary and grammar, which are essential to comprehension. When you begin to think of oral language in terms of communication, social interaction, vocabulary, and grammar, the role it plays in the emergent literacy process suddenly becomes much clearer.

Going back to that delicious blueberry pie again, imagine you've put your apron on, gathered your mixing bowls, utensils, ingredients, and spices. But when you get out your recipe you realize that you don't fully comprehend what it says. Maybe it's the vocabulary that is used, or you're just not familiar with the words. It's going to be difficult to create a delicious blueberry pie if you can't read and comprehend the recipe.

For example, many of my grandmother's recipes used the word *oleo* and some of her measurements were in a shorthand I wasn't familiar with. Of course, a quick Internet search led me to the definition of *oleo* in two seconds flat, but my point is that a lack of vocabulary and comprehension can really hold your students back when it comes to reading. Without strong oral language skills, the emergent literacy process cannot properly function. The development of oral language skills has a profound impact on children's preparedness for kindergarten and on their success throughout their academic career (National Early Literacy Panel, 2008).

You may think you already teach oral language skills to the children in your classroom because you talk to them every single day and allow them to talk with each other. That would be an incorrect assumption; it's almost like saying, "I read to my students each day, surely they'll be reading by the end of the year." It takes careful and intentional planning to successfully support your students in their development of oral language skills.

At this point, you may be thinking, "But Vanessa, there are so many things we have to teach to our kids these days! Adding just one more thing to my already overflowing plate is going to be the straw that broke the camel's back!" But before you give up and fill out that application for the big box store *(again!)*, I want you to know that you *can* provide your students with rich oral language opportunities every day if you're willing to adopt a growth mindset and possibly even reframe your thinking.

Of all the students I've taught over the years, none illustrates the importance of oral language more than Thien. When I first met Thien he was an extremely quiet and shy three-year-old boy. With a late summer birthday, he barely made the cutoff for entrance to our public pre-K program. Native Vietnamese speakers, Thien and his family didn't speak English at home. Not speaking English didn't worry me at all because the majority of my students were dual language learners.

What set Thien apart from his classmates, though, was his quiet nature. By October, Thien still hadn't made an attempt to utter a single word in class, including his own name. This wasn't cause for alarm because many dual language learners go through a "silent period" where they don't yet produce but are actively processing their new language (Saville-Troike, 1988). Thien's classmates often helped him communicate and seemed to magically understand what he was feeling and thinking.

One day I witnessed an amazing display of empathy from another student in the cafeteria who was standing behind Thien in the lunch line. The staff in the cafeteria were used to Thien not speaking, so they would often place food on his tray for him. This day, however, Thien's friend spoke up on his behalf and said to the lunch server, "He doesn't like chicken, he wants a potato." It was definitely one of those moments that reminded me why I loved working with young children.

As the months passed, I held parent conferences with Thien's parents on three separate occasions. Through a translator, they said their son loved coming to school each day and often sang songs at home that he had learned at school. At this point, I knew Thien was going to be fine, he just needed more time. He eventually started nodding when I asked him yes or no questions, which was a huge step in the right direction. I accepted the fact that he needed more time, but nonetheless I still worried about sending him off to kindergarten not speaking.

The following year, on the first day of school in August, I had just finished welcoming a new group of enthusiastic and energetic students to my pre-K classroom and sent them home, one by one, via the agonizingly slow pickup line. I was (once again) sitting at the tiny table in my classroom cutting out name cards with pictures for each of my new students when I heard someone quickly approaching my classroom door. I looked up and saw one of the kindergarten teachers standing in the doorway. This wasn't a usual occurrence since her classroom wasn't located in the pre-K wing of the school building. We exchanged pleasantries for a moment, then she revealed the real reason why she was in my classroom. "What's up with Thien?" she asked. I felt a pit at the bottom of my stomach and I instantly began to apologize, "I worked so hard to get him to talk, but he just wasn't ready," I explained quickly. She looked puzzled at my response and replied, "What are you talking about? I'm asking why he talks so much!"

You know that scene in *Rocky* where he reaches the top of the stairs and the music is playing in the background? Yeah, that was exactly how I felt at that very moment. I laughed long and hard and then finally explained the situation to her. She invited me to her classroom the following day to talk with Thien, so I could see his incredible progress for myself.

When I arrived in her kindergarten classroom the following day, Thien glanced up at me, waved, and shouted "Hi, Mrs. Levin!" loudly from across the room. You could have knocked me down with a feather. I went over to where Thien was working with pattern blocks and I chatted with him for a moment. He told me about the ice cream truck that had visited his neighborhood each day that summer, in addition to what seemed like a million other facts in just a matter of minutes. When I left, he went back to his pattern blocks and continued chatting with his new classmates. Although he hadn't spoken while he was in my classroom, Thien had obviously been absorbing his new language by listening to our stories and songs, as well as his classmates. Although Thien's story was not the norm, it demonstrates the importance of creating a supportive environment for oral language skills to develop.

It doesn't matter if your students are monolingual or you've never had a student who speaks another language in your classroom. My point with this story is that if you build the right foundation for oral language, your students will thrive. In Chapter 16 we'll discuss exactly how you can create a solid foundation for oral language development in your own classroom.

Chapter 16
Where to Start with Oral Language

Oral language is my favorite component of the emergent literacy process because it is so easy to make space in your daily routine for rich oral language opportunities. You can support oral language development during math, science, centers, recess, snack, circle time—any time! But just because it's easy to plan doesn't mean you'll automatically do it. As a teacher dedicated to the success of all your students, it is imperative that you plan and structure your classroom time to help your students develop strong oral language skills.

The easiest place to start when it comes to oral language is center time. As you're probably aware, though, every teacher has different ideas about center time and what it should look like. Sometimes these ideas come from other teachers who have shared what they do in their classrooms, from social media, or even from administrators. I'm going to be very clear, so listen up: center time is too important to leave up to the teacher next door, social media, or anybody who may not have a background in early childhood education. The three main benefits of center time are:

Oral language development

Self-regulation

Social skills

Anything else that is learned during center time is icing on the cake. Because this book is all about literacy, we won't focus specifically on self-regulation or social skills, although I do have plenty of resources that address these skills in the Teaching Trailblazers.

Now that we've got that out of the way, how can you use center time to develop oral language skills? The best way to support the development of oral language skills during center time is to provide your students with large blocks of uninterrupted time to play. While they're playing, they're talking to their friends. The way children talk to one another during centers is spontaneous and child initiated. This means that children are talking to one another for the purpose of communicating their thoughts and ideas. The way children speak to one another during center time is entirely different from the way they speak with us as adults during large-group or even small-group instructional time. The conversations we, as teachers, have with children in the classroom are predominantly teacher initiated (adult to student) and directed (Dickinson, & Tabors, 2001).

TIME SPENT IN CENTERS

Now it's time to discuss the length of time for centers, because this is a critical piece of the oral language puzzle. Having uninterrupted time for centers means not signaling that children should clean up and move on to a designated center at predetermined intervals. This practice is often referred to as forced rotation. I've mentored many teachers who used this method and they were all well intentioned. They often justified their use of forced rotation as the only way to ensure that each child gets a turn at every center every day. However, if we revisit the true purpose of center time, it isn't about having each child visit every center each day. Forced rotation during center time leads to frustration on the part of the children and very little time for rich discussions to take place. When young children have uninterrupted time to engage in play with their peers, more rich conversations will take place, resulting in more opportunities for oral language skills to develop.

FORCED ROTATION OF CENTERS

Here's an adult example of what forced rotation feels like for children. Imagine there's a new movie you want to see. You discover that this movie is playing in a theater near you, so you purchase your tickets in advance. When you get to the theater you get a big tub of buttery popcorn and a soda and head toward your theater. After you find your seat, you settle in and start munching on your popcorn as you watch the previews. Finally, after an agonizing 20 minutes, the movie finally begins. This movie is everything you'd hoped it would be and more. Then, in the middle of a pivotal scene, the house lights abruptly go on, the movie is stopped, and an usher enters the theater, clapping his hands and telling you it's time to go to another theater to see a different movie. You're so confused: you wanted to see *this* movie, you liked *this* movie, and you're not at all interested in the movie playing in the next theater! Despite your protests, the usher shoos you out the door and hustles you into the next theater. You sit down in the next theater to watch a movie that is totally unappealing to you—perhaps with loud explosions, weapons, and fast cars—not your idea of a good movie at all! Then the usher appears again and forces you to go to yet another theater. Are you with me so far?

That leads to the next logical question: What do successful, self-directed centers infused with opportunities for rich oral language development look like in action? To illustrate, I'd like to introduce you to a cheerful and outgoing preschooler named Elena. One morning, after Elena had hung up her unicorn backpack and signed in, she made a beeline for our center time choice board. The choice board was just a piece of poster board with photos of each center glued to the front and laminated. Although it may not have looked like much, for Elena and the rest of my students the choice board was a tool they used to map out their time spent in centers. This day, Elena studied the board intently, scanning the pictures as if she were searching for treasure. Finally, she placed the index finger of her right hand squarely on one photo—the art center.

As Elena settled into our whole-group meeting area, I overheard her telling a few of her friends about the picture she was going to make for her mother in the art center that day. It turns out that it was her mother's birthday, and Elena wanted to make something special for her during center time. After our morning ritual had concluded and it was time for centers to begin, the students trickled over to the choice board to make their plans for the play. Elena was way ahead of them. She headed straight for the art center and stared at the shelf that held many different types of paper, searching for just the right color. As she selected a piece of pale blue paper and picked up a crayon caddy, I noticed that her friends from earlier had also started to gather in the art center. It turns out, they wanted to make pictures for their mothers too.

For the next 50 minutes or so, Elena and her friends sat around the circular table in the art center sharing crayons, markers, glue, and a wide variety of other collage materials. As they worked on their masterpieces, they asked each other for turns with different colored markers and crayons. "Look!" exclaimed Sophia, "I found this sticker of a puppy, does your mom like dogs?" The girls chose to spend their entire center time in this area. Occasionally another child would wander over and ask them what they were doing, and the girls happily explained their plan. A few of the other children even stayed and created their own picture, but nowhere near as long as Elena and her group.

When their pictures were elaborate and embellished with a multitude of stickers, sequins, and feathers, I wandered over and picked up a book that was on display in the art center. The book was a collection of famous paintings; I showed them how the artists had signed their names to some of the paintings to tell the world who had created the art. Two of the girls got their name cards out of our name chart and began to dutifully write their names. Elena and one of the others attempted to write their names without the extra support of the name card.

The amount of learning that took place during center time that day was incredible. The girls in the art center were engaged in a single activity for almost an entire hour. They self-selected their own center and practiced self-regulation skills by taking turns with the various art supplies. They communicated with one another in a very relaxed and informal way all throughout this time. They exercised their fine motor skills as they cut, glued, and even wrote their names. That day's center time was a success.

You might be afraid that your students will miss out on other center experiences if they choose to spend the full allotted time at just one center...but just think about the rich oral language, fine motor, and other experiences Elena and her friends would have missed if I'd rung a bell after 20 minutes and they had to leave their beautiful creations unfinished! In your classroom, your centers will be more successful when you allow children the freedom to follow their own interests. When you know and understand the true purpose of centers, you'll be supporting your students in a way that will help them develop crucial skills they will need for the rest of their lives, including oral language.

ORAL LANGUAGE AND VOCABULARY DEVELOPMENT IN CENTERS

The dramatic play center is the perfect example of a center that naturally facilitates the development of oral language, self-regulation, and social skills. One of our Teaching Trailblazers members, Andrea, noticed huge gains in her student's vocabulary when she started being more intentional about supporting oral language development in her dramatic play center.

I started infusing new vocabulary words in the dramatic play center. For example, when asking the chef in the dramatic play center about the pizza they're making for their customers I may ask, "What toppings does your customer want on the pizza?" Many students may not know that the items they put on the pizza are called toppings. Or I may ask a baker what ingredients they need to make the cookies their customer ordered. Or what recipe they will use to make a pie. Using unfamiliar vocabulary and using it continuously helps build oral language skills.

In this example, Andrea was scaffolding to support her student's oral language and vocabulary development. Scaffolding is a way for you to provide your students with guided support as they begin to learn new vocabulary and develop oral language skills. Here's what another member, Jennifer, experienced when she started scaffolding in her own classroom:

My biggest win has been realizing how important scaffolding can be for improving oral language. I used to just let them talk at center time and I thought that was enough, but when I started scaffolding, I was amazed at how much their vocabulary and oral language improved!

When you begin to intentionally support oral language development in each center, your students will immediately benefit from your efforts. One Trailblazers member, Kieley, experienced this in her own classroom:

> Since joining, I started using your dramatic play kits and being more intentional about how I set it up and introduced it. It was thrilling to see my children excel in their oral language abilities so quickly. I was surprised to see such a high return on activities that required relatively little preparation. So excited to continue to improve in this area!

Oral language development isn't limited to the dramatic play center; here's what happened when Trailblazers member Cynthia created a rich oral language experience for her students in the sand and water area.

> Last week I turned the sand and water table into a bath center for the baby dolls for our family unit. The children were talking just like mommies and daddies would with the babies—it was so cute, but also a great way to naturally build oral language skills.

Another Trailblazers member, Karen, offered an extremely helpful piece of advice about how her sensory table is facilitating oral language development.

> Sometimes simple things like placing your sensory table away from the wall will encourage more peer-to-peer conversations because the students can stand at the table face to face as opposed to playing side by side.

The bottom line is that when we give children time to explore the centers they're most interested in, you're allowing time for oral language development, self-regulation, and social skills to develop.

READING ALOUD

Of course, there are many other ways to infuse your early childhood class-room with rich opportunities for oral language and vocabulary development. At the very beginning of the year I like to explore wordless picture books with my students. It may seem contrary to use wordless picture books to teach vocabulary and oral language, but they're perfect for helping young children verbalize their thoughts about what they see in the pictures. Here's what Jim Trelease, author of *The Read-Aloud Handbook*, had to say about wordless picture books when I interviewed him in 2013:

> Wordless books are a wonderful introduction to books and plotting for children who can't yet read. Since we become picture-literate before we become print-literate, they can "read" the book if someone helps them blaze a trail through the narrative initially. After hearing the book and seeing how the clues for the narrative are in the pictures or illustrations, the child can pretend to read, though in fact they are taking real steps in reading. Just as pilots "read" the sky ahead of them (no words, just images of clouds), the child is taking a reading on the plot from the illustrations.

MULTIPLE READINGS OF THE SAME STORY

Another way to support vocabulary development through reading books aloud is to read the same book multiple times. Word learning requires many exposures over an extended period. With each additional exposure, the word may become incrementally closer to being fully learned (Neuman & Wright, 2014). Of course, the books you choose to read multiple times need to be fun, interactive, and engaging—otherwise you'll lose their attention. I like to read different versions of the same fairy tale over the course of one or two weeks. The basic structure of the story remains the same, but the multiple versions invite more discussion and rich vocabulary as we compare and contrast the basic story with the different versions. Think of Cinderella stories from different cultures around the globe, for example. *Adelita* by Tomie dePaola, *The Korean Cinderella* by Shirley Climo, *Yeh-Shen: A Cinderella Story from China* by Ai-Ling Louie, *Mufaro's Beautiful Daughters* by John Steptoe, and *The Rough-Face Girl* by Rafe Martin are just a few of the hundreds of versions of the Cinderella story out there!

To take it one step further and make learning oral language and vocabulary even more fun and playful, you can have students act out the fairy tales or stories you read multiple times. I like to start on Monday by reading a classic version of the fairy tale, then I read different versions of the same fairy tale on the subsequent days. Finally, on the fifth day the children are so familiar with the characters and plot that they're ready to act it out.

The first time we act out the story of The Three Little Pigs, I always narrate and invite the children to join in as much as possible to help with the narration. I also scaffold as I narrate, for example, "The first little pig was lazy, and he said..." Finally, I invite a student to narrate, while still standing by for support if necessary. The vocabulary my students learn from just one fairy tale is tremendous. When I hear them telling each other, "You're lazy, like the first little pig!" then I know they've gained valuable oral language and vocabulary skills. But it might be time to work on those social skills!

Here's what Summer, another member of the Teaching Trailblazers, had to say about her experience with multiple readings of the same book.

> When reading a book, sometimes I ask open-ended questions such as, "What do you think this book is about?" "What do you think will happen next?" I noticed that when I read the same book the second time and asked the same questions again, the children came up with more interesting and complete responses."

There are so many opportunities to infuse oral language and vocabulary development, this chapter could be an entire book if we were to cover them all. What I hope you take away from this chapter is that oral language isn't something you have to teach "in addition" to everything else, you just need to be intentional and weave opportunities for learning throughout each day.

In Chapter 17 you'll learn how to make oral language skills hands on and enticing for your students. In addition, you'll discover the two centers that are the biggest powerhouses of oral language development and how to make them work in your classroom.

Chapter 17
Oral Language Reflection

Out of the four different steps, oral language is the one that lends itself most naturally to the HEART method. Oral language already exists in your classroom; you just need to make the time and space for it to occur. With just a few minor adjustments you can easily apply the HEART method to support the development of oral language skills in your own classroom.

Before we begin, let's review the HEART method one last time:

Hands-on

Enticing

A connection

Repeated exposure

Time for practice daily

Hands-on: It may seem contrary to use hands-on methods to teach oral language skills, but it's really quite simple, and it may even be something you're already doing in your classroom. Aside from dramatic play, there are a few other centers that are powerhouses of oral language learning. Two of these centers are the storytelling center (or flannel board) and the puppet theater. Storytelling and puppets offer young children a supportive structure to practice their oral language skills. Retelling familiar or favorite stories using flannel or magnetic pieces gives children an opportunity to use their hands to manipulate the pieces, which makes the experience so much more fun and engaging. Puppets are an especially fun and playful way to develop oral language skills. Young children will experiment more with language when they play with puppets.

Enticing: Ask any preschooler and they're likely to tell you that they love playing, and the dramatic play center is all about play—it says so right in the name. When you intentionally incorporate opportunities that facilitate oral language into your dramatic play area, you're creating an environment that will entice your students to practice and expand their oral language skills.

One way to set your students up for oral language success in the dramatic play center and get them talking is to facilitate scenarios that are most familiar to them. For example, a grocery store may be more familiar to your students than an airport. Think about how many times your students have been to the grocery store as opposed to an airport. Your students will have more language skills they can build on when you set up a grocery store in your dramatic play center. That doesn't mean you can never set up an airport scenario in your dramatic play center; it just means you may want to wait until much later in the year when your students have had more time to practice those familiar scenarios. This is especially true with children who have language delays or those who are dual language learners.

A connection: When you allow young children to take the lead and follow their own interests at center time, they will naturally make their own personal connections. The girls in Chapter 16 who were making pictures for their mothers were all highly motivated. Not only that, they were practicing their oral language skills in context, with a very authentic purpose.

Repeated exposure: You've got this! Daily center time with self-selection of centers by your students is the easiest way to offer repeated exposure. High-quality picture books with rich vocabulary read multiple times will also go a long way to develop oral language skills.

Time: You can easily make more time for oral language development during center time. You can also add wordless picture books into some of your read-aloud sessions to practice telling a story using the pictures.

When you understand the importance of these activities, it should be easy to accomplish this final step of the HEART method.

Once you've applied the HEART method to oral language in your classroom, you may find the most difficult piece of this step is reflection. It can be more difficult to measure the success of your efforts when it comes to oral language.

REFLECTION

As you begin to reflect on the information shared in Step 4, take time to stop and think about what you're already doing that follows the HEART method. There's no need to completely change everything you're doing in your classroom. In fact,

I'm willing to bet you're already doing some of these things outlined in Step 4. Take a moment to write down the things you're already doing. When you write your reflections on paper, they become more meaningful and allow you to see the progress you're making or have already made more clearly.

CHALLENGE

Next, I challenge you to identify just one thing you learned in Step 4 that you're not already doing in your classroom. Choose a new objective or practice that feels doable to you. If you choose something that's a big departure from the way you normally teach, you'll quickly become overwhelmed and discouraged. Remember, the most effective changes take place slowly, over time.

SELF-ASSESSMENT

After you have made that one small change in your classroom, stop and ask yourself the following questions:

How did it go?

How did it make me feel?

Is there anything I want to change or do differently next time?

TROUBLESHOOTING

If you've ever struggled to incorporate puppets for storytelling into your centers, you're not alone. Here's what one of our Teaching Trailblazers members recently reported about her experience with using puppets during center time:

> I had to put my puppet theater away for safety reasons. All the kids did was chase each other around the classroom with the puppets, roaring like animals and trying to bite each other. Any advice?

When I was an instructional specialist traveling from classroom to classroom across more than 10 different campuses to support pre-K teachers, I noticed that puppet theaters were often absent from the classrooms I visited. When asked, some teachers said their students weren't using them, so they got rid of them, and others said it was too noisy or took up too much space.

When children aren't visiting a center it's not always a sign that they aren't interested. I encourage you to think about a few things before writing off your puppet theater once and for all.

Modeling: Whenever children aren't using materials in the way you intended for them to be used, or in ways that could be dangerous or disruptive to others, it's always a good idea to go back and model what properly using those materials looks like. Model it for your students, then invite them to model it for you, and finally invite them to practice while you observe.

Introduction: How did you introduce the puppet center to your students? So often we take for granted that children inherently know things they really don't know. For example, how to use puppets is a completely foreign concept for most young children. When you introduce your puppet center, include some instruction about the purpose of the center in addition to how to use the puppets.

Types of puppets: This one is a big ah-ha moment for many teachers: if you put puppets in your puppet center like lions, dinosaurs, cows, or pigs, think about what these puppets all have in common. They're all animals that make noise. It only makes sense that students would chase each other around while mimicking the sounds and behaviors of the animals. Instead, just provide a few puppets that go along with one story or song at a time. For example, if you're reading the fairy tale *Goldilocks and the Three Bears* you might place a girl puppet and three bear puppets in your puppet center. Your students will be familiar with the fairy tale because it's one you've read to them multiple times. When you include puppets for a specific story or song, you're offering your students a supportive structure in which to practice oral language and setting them up for success. Save the dinosaurs, lions, and other animals for later, once you have a context for those puppets.

Adding books for retelling: In addition to adding puppets for one story or song to your puppet center, you can also add a copy of the corresponding book. The addition of the book will offer your students extra support as they retell the story in the book using puppets.

Having an audience: What's the point of a puppet show without an audience? Encourage your students to recruit an "audience" to watch their puppet shows. When there's an audience present the puppeteers will be practicing expressive language, and the audience will be practicing receptive language skills.

As an aside, having a classroom puppet that the teacher uses exclusively to increase engagement and introduce concepts to students is not the same as having a puppet theater in your classroom. These are two entirely different things used for different purposes.

Another center that can be problematic for some teachers is the flannel or magnetic storytelling area. Storytelling with flannel and magnet boards is such a powerful tool for developing oral language skills. Here's what Analise experienced in her classroom when she opened up her flannel board center for the first time.

> I remember having a flannel board in my classroom when I was in preschool and I was so excited to have one in my own classroom my first year teaching. I spent the summer making my own flannel sets and cutting out all the pieces by hand. I had each set in a zippered plastic bag, ready to go the first week of school. But when I opened the center it was a hot mess! The pieces I had so painstakingly crafted were ruined and lost in the first five minutes. I was so upset that I put the flannel board in my closet. Help!

You probably won't be surprised that my suggestions for Analise are similar to the suggestions I made for the puppet center.

Model: When it comes to the flannel or magnet board center, you'll want to use it in your large-group lessons for several weeks to help your children understand what it is and the purpose it serves. Remember, most young children don't have a flannel or magnet board storytelling center in their homes, so this will be their first exposure to it.

Introduction: The first story you should put at this center should be one your students are familiar with and that you have read to them multiple times. A good example would be a fairy tale or a nursery rhyme. This will increase interest, engagement, and confidence.

Number of sets: When you're ready to open this center for your students to use, be sure to put only one story at the flannel board so you don't end up with mixed up sets.

Adding books for retelling: Just like with the puppet center, you'll also want to add a copy of the book that goes along with your flannel story to provide your students with a supportive structure for retelling.

Having an audience: Retelling a story with puppets or on a flannel board is a performance. Without an audience, there's not as much motivation to perform. Allow your students to "recruit" audience members to watch them retell the story at the flannel or magnet board.

By following the HEART method for developing oral language skills and by engaging in continuous reflection, you'll continue to fine tune your skills as a teacher...and your students will continue to thrive.

You're welcome to try out the ideas and suggestions in this chapter on your own, but if you would like more guidance and support, you're invited to join other passionate early childhood educators in our free Oral Language Challenge. You can find out more about the challenge at https://www.pre-kpages.com/TeachSmarter, along with additional information and resources for infusing your classroom with rich oral language opportunities all year long.

In the next chapter, you'll be introduced to several teachers who have experienced amazing transformations in their teaching practice as a result of implementing many of the strategies we've covered in this book so far.

Chapter 18
Case Studies

In this chapter I'd like to introduce you to some of the members of the Teaching Trailblazers as they openly share their experiences and the results they have achieved in their own classrooms.

You'll meet:

AnneMarie, a veteran special educator with 30 years of experience, who shares how she rediscovered her passion for teaching and improved her performance evaluations at the same time.

Jennifer, a teacher of 16 years, who shares how her membership in the Teaching Trailblazers helped her campus achieve national accreditation.

Lisa, who, for the first time in 14 years, stopped taking work home and didn't need to do any prep on the weekends. She was even able to leave work an hour earlier each day!

MEET ANNEMARIE

For more than 30 years, AnneMarie has dedicated her professional life to teaching pre-K children with special educational needs. She loves to see her children—many of whom are Hispanic and from monolingual homes—surpass expectations and build the skills they need to succeed.

The Challenge: Feeling Defeated and Ready to Walk Away from Teaching for Good

Four years ago, AnneMarie had lost her love for teaching. A demanding new curriculum and evaluation system had dropped on her desk. She was expected to prepare her children for a regular classroom, even though they had language challenges and special needs. She just didn't know where to start—which left her feeling isolated and frustrated.

In particular, she couldn't find the recipe for reading success. Years of traditional English as a second language training had taught her that children with other languages struggled with phonological awareness; and they wouldn't grasp concepts such as rhyming or breaking words into syllables. AnneMarie couldn't see a way to break through.

As poor evaluations piled up, AnneMarie felt short on training, short on support—and ready to quit teaching for good.

> I was having all kinds of problems. I was ready to walk out, stop being a teacher. I didn't have any love for it anymore. I was just done with what they were trying to make the kids do.

The Solution: Putting the Positivity Back in Her Classroom

AnneMarie was already no stranger to Pre-K Pages. But she'd only downloaded the occasional teaching resource from the site. That all changed when she attended a luncheon hosted by founder Vanessa Levin. Inspired by her enthusiasm and expertise, AnneMarie immediately signed up for the Trailblazers.

Where she'd previously felt lost, suddenly she found lots of the answers she'd been looking for. She watched Vanessa's "power hour" and "office hours" training videos over and over. And she felt supermotivated to try out things she'd previously thought were way over her students' heads.

She learned tips and techniques to support her students' reading. And she reached out to the community's trail guides—other veteran teachers who just love to show you the way.

She felt the joy coming back and threw all the negativity she'd heard about special education right out the window.

AnneMarie packed her classroom with ideas and materials she'd learned and sourced from the Trailblazers. She downloaded step-by-step lesson plans, which saved precious planning time and made learning fun. She created engaging learning centers throughout the classroom, which gave the children more variety and got them excited about literacy, math, and science. And she used materials that supported reading in a modern way, including pocket charts, syllable clapping and fun rhyming games.

You name it, AnneMarie was using it!

> There are so many components to the Trailblazers site. In addition to all the resources, having a community of other preschool teachers that you can talk to is amazing. The whole thing has been amazing.

The Result: Remarkable Improvements in Reading—and Her Retirement on Hold

Within hours of hitting play on Vanessa's ideas-packed training videos, AnneMarie felt her joy for teaching return. When she put what she'd learned into practice, the results were remarkable. The site's phonological materials and games set off an amazing transformation in her children. Suddenly her three-year-olds were pointing to the right letters and thriving. It was so inspiring for AnneMarie to see their faces light up as they learned. Pocket charts, designed to teach concepts of print, were being obsessively followed by the kids. They were recognizing words—and enjoying learning in a way they never had before.

Other ideas, such as using clothespins and dot stickers to improve the children's motor skills, were a big success. Although many of them had only been comfortable manipulating phones and tablets at home, now they were holding pencils better, drawing smarter pictures, and honing vital skills. As her children flourished, so did AnneMarie's evaluations. Her scores shot up and she was getting consistent ratings of exemplary or excellent.

AnneMarie's dread of going into work every day is no more. Instead, she approaches every day with confidence. With prepared, step-by-step teaching resources on tap, she feels she can achieve so much more. As her class thrives, AnneMarie has more of her life back. She can download all the resources and lesson plans she needs in minutes. So when she leaves for the day, the whole night is hers.

> The Teaching Trailblazers has been mind-blowing and has changed my teaching life. It has turned me completely around—so to heck with retirement!

AnneMarie is no longer thinking about retirement. She's rediscovered her passion for teaching and plans to keep encouraging a love of learning in her students for years to come.

MEET JEN

Jen has been teaching pre-K for the past 16 years and she's been loyal to the same corporate learning center for all that time. Jen has an associate's degree in early childhood education and is a passionate lifelong learner who loves to see her kids make progress.

The Challenge: Whole Weekends Lost to Lesson Planning and Longing to Give More to Her Students

Jen is the type of teacher every parent wants for their kids. Although some are just there for the paycheck, it's a total vocation for her. But digging for the fun materials and ideas her kids would love was also digging into her life.

Planning lessons took up whole weekends, leaving zero time for herself. She was spending chunks of time—and her own money—setting up her dramatic play center, creating her own resources, printing pictures, and laminating them.

There was another challenge, too. For the first time, she had a student in class who spoke no English, just Polish. And Jen had no idea how to help. With no free time to enjoy life, and gaps in her learning that she simply didn't know how to fill, Jen felt frustrated and exhausted.

I was planning all the time on my weekends—which left me with no free time. I also had one student that I had no idea how to help. I was stressed out and didn't know what to do.

The Solution: All the Teaching Materials She Could Ever Need and a Community That Helps and Inspires Her

Checkmated by the challenge of her nonnative student, Jen reached out to Vanessa via her popular Facebook page. Jen was so thrilled with the advice she received, she signed up to become a Trailblazer. Her membership unlocked instant access to a vast Teaching Resource Vault of learning materials, including dramatic play kits and thematic lesson plans for math and literacy. Jen could print and laminate complete lesson plans for the full year ahead. There were so many printable activities that she didn't need to look anywhere else. And videos were available 24/7 that offered practical, actionable training.

Jen loved the unique community of pre-K Trailblazers from around the world. As a person who loves to give, she began to share her advice. And whenever she had a question about her own classroom, there were enthusiastic, passionate teachers right there to help her.

The Result: More Free Time—and Transforming Her New Skills and Knowledge into a 97% Accreditation Score

With the Teaching Resource Vault at her fingertips, Jen can now do all her planning during nap time. Which means she's finally got her weekends—and her life—back.

When Jen's mom was ill recently, her newfound free time came into its own. Instead of wasted weekends of work, she could spend precious time with her family.

Although classroom challenges used to leave her feeling lost and frustrated, she now gets instant support and answers in the community. It's helped her connect with like-minded teachers, who want to do just as well as she does.

The Trailblazer's masterclass training videos have supercharged her teaching skills to such a level that she has become a mentor to other teachers on her campus. Jen also credits the Teaching Trailblazers for helping her ace a recent national accreditation visit. The assessors were so wowed by her interactions with pupils, and the engaging materials she was using, they marked her at 97%!

> Without Pre-K Pages I'd be a lot more stressed. I don't have to spend my weekends planning, so I can spend more time with my family. And that means the most to me.

MEET LISA

Lisa is an elementary school teacher, with more than two decades of experience supporting young children at the start of their learning journey.

The Challenge: Overwhelmed and Burnt Out after Being Dropped in the Deep End with Pre-K Reassignment

Lisa had the shock of her life when, after 25 years teaching first grade and kindergarten, her school district restructured its resources and reassigned her to pre-K for the very first time.

Although she'd always felt confident and at ease with her teaching, suddenly she was like a deer in headlights. She was asked to change buildings and switch to a much smaller classroom than she'd been used to. And when the new school year started, the struggle and stress only got worse.

She'd assumed at least some of the kindergarten activities she was familiar with would work with younger kids. But they all fell flat. Her colleagues gave her a pacing guide, but not the practical teaching materials to support it. So, it fell on Lisa to endlessly trawl the Web for suitable resources, which quickly took over her life. Most nights she was up until 10 p.m. prepping for the next morning—and weekends were just as hectic. There was no let up, no space to breathe—just a full-on, unrelenting workload. She could feel herself burning out, as her job overwhelmed her life. She had no time for her husband, her son, or herself.

> I was working way too hard, spending ridiculous amounts of time searching and prepping for classes—and I was just so worn out. I didn't have a life and my husband was like, "who are you?" I realized I had to figure out how to do this or maybe this wasn't the grade for me.

The Solution: Taking Back Control of Her Job and Her Life by Joining the Teaching Trailblazers

Lisa made it her mission to take control of the spiraling situation. While looking around for new ideas and support, she discovered the Pre-K Pages website. She loved their overarching message—that it is possible to teach better and save time—and started investing in individual learning packages to see how they worked in her classroom.

The more materials she used, the more Lisa fell in love with Pre-K Pages. She began reading Pre-K founder Vanessa Levin's blog avidly and soon signed up for the Trailblazers. Lisa's Teaching Trailblazer membership gave her access to an entire vault of time-saving teaching and planning resources. She downloaded materials for all kinds of areas she'd been struggling with, from math to literacy, rhymes and themes—and everything in between. Lisa particularly loves the Trailblazer pacing guide. It gives her a clear plan to follow for every week of the school year and suggests age-appropriate book lists and resources. So she doesn't have to search for herself anymore.

She also uses her membership to take charge of her professional development. Whenever Lisa encounters a new challenge in the classroom—from getting kids started writing to having challenging conversations with the principal—there's a video tutorial or Q&A available on demand, offering powerful advice that helps her do her job better.

The Trailblazer community has given Lisa another outlet to troubleshoot challenges and share her successes, so she never feels like she's struggling alone.

> The Teaching Trailblazer has given me a game plan, a structure, and the resources to be a better teacher. And everything works together seamlessly.

The Result: Weeks of Her Life Back, a Soaring Skill Set, and Resources Her Colleagues Envy

Lisa says Teaching Trailblazers has become the "spinal cord" for her classroom. Saying it's been a game changer would be an understatement. Because it's actually been a life changer!

With a clear plan for her classroom, and instant access to every resource she needs, she can now do virtually all her prep during nap time. And it's not unusual for her to be fully prepped two weeks ahead. For someone who'd previously been losing every night and every weekend to work, it feels like the difference between night and day.

Now, when she heads home, she can enjoy her family, and her life. She's even found time to paint her toenails during the week again! Lisa literally has gotten weeks of free time back every year, with no compromise on the quality of her teaching.

The Trailblazer pacing guide has created more consistency and clarity to her teaching, which the kids love. Parents, colleagues, and even her principal have all commented on how organized she is now, and she's seeing her kids make progress faster than before.

The site's practical and actionable video training has helped develop Lisa's skills and confidence—and really get a grip on the nuances of teaching pre-K. After a bumpy start to teaching at a brand-new grade, Lisa now has the confidence to bring her "A" game every single day. Stress and struggle have been replaced with satisfaction and stability thanks to her Trailblazer membership.

I hope that these stories inspired you. In Chapter 19 you'll learn the five habits of highly effective teachers and the secret recipe that helped one overwhelmed, exhausted, and isolated teacher become more confident and content.

Chapter 19
What's Next?

At my three-city tour to meet with and support early childhood educators in 2019, one of my stops was in Detroit. We met at the movie theater to attend the premiere of *A Beautiful Day in the Neighborhood*. After the movie, several of us went out for dinner and I got to catch up with a long-time acquaintance named Heather. Heather is an in-home childcare provider who has been faithfully executing new techniques, deepening her understanding of early childhood development, and staying connected with a community of pre-K professionals for several years.

As typically happens at these gatherings, the conversation over dinner turned to our classrooms. Instead of bringing problems for other teachers to help troubleshoot, though, this time Heather stepped up as a voice of wisdom and experience. She listened attentively as other pre-K teachers talked about their classroom management challenges or posed questions about literacy development for their students. Then she offered practical solutions and gave helpful advice based on research-based "best practices." I couldn't help reflecting on my earlier interactions with Heather, where the shoe had been clearly on the other foot.

As dinner wound up, my curiosity got the best of me. "Heather," I said. "You are such a pro now! Not that you weren't already a dedicated teacher before, but I have to know: What has changed?"

Heather leaned in and smiled. "You know what, Vanessa? I finally *feel* like a pro. I'm so happy now. At the start of every weekend, I silently give thanks for the exciting learning that's unfolding among my students, and for the culture we've built. Then I close the door to my supply closet, leave the teaching materials I've already prepped in their place on the shelves, and I don't open that door again until Monday morning shortly before the kids arrive. I'm a better teacher than I've ever been, but I'm not overworked anymore. I have the confidence that my students are on track for kindergarten readiness, and it allows me to relax and have more fun with them. I never thought I'd see this day, but now I'm *exactly* the teacher I always wanted to be."

I know there are teachers who will read Heather's story and wonder, *What's the secret recipe she discovered? How can I channel some of that magic?* After all, Heather's story is vastly different from the experience of most teachers I meet for the first time.

Most teachers start their careers with an abundance of energy—they faithfully plan their lessons every evening while also juggling dinner preparation and wading through the minefield of their own children's bedtimes. They scour the Internet for ideas every day, nearly go broke spending money at the dollar store, and are always on the lookout for the perfect activity to help aid their students in having "lightbulb moments" in their learning.

As time goes by, though, teachers start to wear down. Their initial energy and enthusiasm begin to dry up as they're handed an ever-growing list of standards they have to teach . . . with new requirements handed down by their administrators every year. Eventually, many of these well-intentioned teachers start to wonder, *Is this all there is?* Many will reach a point of burnout and may even consider leaving the classroom for good. The pressure is too great, and the rewards seem to diminish as time goes on. Oh—and don't forget the siren song of the higher paycheck they'd get by switching careers.

One of my goals, as a mentor and advisor to *thousands* of teachers over the last 20 years, is to elevate the field of early childhood education—to the point where preschool is seen as a vital part of children's educational process. I believe that *all* children deserve a high-quality early childhood education. As a leader, I have dedicated my life to supporting teachers with practical help, community, and inspiration . . . even as they receive a high-quality *teacher* education themselves.

HABITS OF EXCELLENT TEACHERS

Because you've made it this far in the book, here is what I already know about you: You're not content with "teaching as usual." You refuse to settle for the status quo. You're on the lookout for fresh ideas but also time-honored best practices you can infuse into your teaching, so you can continue sharpening your skills as an early childhood educator of *excellence*. You don't just want your students to continue into kindergarten and beyond; you want them to shine.

So, what are the keys to becoming the best educator you can be? Not surprisingly, they don't typically come in the form of earth-shattering fault lines in your classroom, when you power through every single moment of every single day, or *finally* someone hands you the keys to the Treasure of the Sierra Madre and you soar to Teacher of the Year in a single bound. Here's the secret: you don't have to completely overhaul the way you approach teaching in order to become a stellar teacher.

Consider a home cook. A person doesn't become a master chef by cooking the same recipes over and over again without making any adjustments. Instead, on their quest for greatness, they go through an intensive experience where they master not recipes but *techniques*. Once they have a foundation of strong techniques to use in the kitchen, they can apply those techniques to any recipe they ever follow. Over time, they gain a sort of "muscle memory" that allows them to float through the kitchen with ease. They cook more efficiently. They become more creative. And because they have mastered the proper techniques, they stop relying on recipes at all, and instead follow their intuition as they branch out into new flavor combinations, textures, and sensory experiences. (Okay, now I'm getting hungry.)

Like home cooks, I believe that all teachers have the potential to develop "muscle memory" in the classroom—to rise to the level of master teachers, whose students consistently gain new skills, almost effortlessly! However, teachers *don't* reach this level of proficiency just by scouring social media sites for ideas. It turns out, there are habits you can build into your teaching practice that, when applied over the space of just a few years, will help you achieve more than you've ever achieved in the classroom.

THE FIVE HABITS OF HIGHLY EFFECTIVE TEACHERS

In the book *The 7 Habits of Highly Effective People: Powerful Lessons in Personal Change* (Covey & Covey, 2020), Stephen Covey says:

> Did you ever consider how ridiculous it would be to try to cram on a farm—to forget to plant in the spring, play all summer and then cram in the fall to bring in the harvest? The farm is a natural system. The price must be paid, and the process followed. You always reap what you sow; there is no shortcut.

To transform our teaching, we must adopt certain habits, on an ongoing basis, shared by the most successful teachers. Building the habits of outstanding teachers will save us from the ineffectiveness of trying to "cram" in a feverish, power-through burst of energy at the start of the year, and instead lead to long-term positive change. Quite literally, adopting these habits will transform not just your teaching, but *you* as a leader. So, what are the five habits of highly effective teachers?

HABIT ONE: SET THE RIGHT GOALS

When asked, most teachers will tell you that their goal for their students is to have them kindergarten ready by the end of the year. It's a noble goal—and a great one to have in place. But it's so large in scope, and so vague! What does kindergarten readiness mean, exactly? Does it mean that your students can see and recite 50 sight words? Or that every student checks all the boxes on your state or national standards? I would submit to you this, instead: if your students don't have self-regulation skills, they will struggle in elementary school (and beyond), even if they do show signs of having learned the standards.

As a teacher myself, I know you feel an extreme pressure to get your students meeting the standards by the end of the year, but what you *know* in your heart of hearts is that what the kids *really* need is social-emotional development. It's possible that what you are told to do (by administrators) and what you know your students actually *need* may be two different things. Very rarely do state/national standards take into consideration the social-emotional components of young children's development. Or perhaps some standards do address this, but they are very vague and broad, like "be a good citizen."

It just so happened that the way I naturally taught infused all my teaching with social-emotional learning and helped the students develop self-regulation skills. When I finally realized that other teachers were not experiencing the same results, I had to go back and try to reconstruct exactly what the difference was. It turns out, my "accidental" focus on social-emotional learning was allowing the children the freedom to learn academic subjects in a safe, comfortable environment—and they were flourishing. They felt that they could take academic risks because their social-emotional needs had been met.

Consistently, year after year, most of my students achieved 100% letter recognition by October—it didn't take a full school year—and we were free to start applying their letter recognition to higher-level literacy skills. When I finally incorporated teaching letters and letter sounds at the same time, together, using songs, hand motions, and movements, their learning skyrocketed.

So, if it's not enough to aim for "kindergarten readiness" by the end of the school year, what goals should teachers actually be setting for their students? First, you must be prepared to meet your students' social-emotional needs, they need to have the safety and security provided by rules, routines, and procedures in your classroom for real academic learning to begin. As a teacher, this means you don't wait for a child to start throwing tantrums (or throwing things!) before you start looking for solutions. You cannot afford to be reactive. Instead, excellent teachers start the year with a vision for providing their students with plenty of opportunities for social-emotional learning to occur. When you have a plan in place to facilitate social-emotional growth, you create a safe space for learning for all your students. You will be prepared for the unexpected.

This is where standards and benchmarks miss the mark. They do not take into consideration the fact that if your classroom is total chaos and your students don't have the sense of safety and security that come from routines and procedures in place, they can't meet the standards. Again: the best learning cannot take place until the feeling of safety and security for students is met.

For example, you will likely need to start organizing your students' environment right from day one. You can provide a picture schedule so the children can see what's going to happen next, even if they can't read. By looking at a picture schedule, students can see what has already happened in their day. They will soon understand that when they get to the end of the schedule, they are going home. Children crave a sense of control—and truly, to know that the adults in their lives have a plan in place—so using a simple picture schedule helps them feel like they have control over their surroundings: at any time, they can see the schedule and understand the progress they're making toward the end of the day.

Another wonderful preliminary goal for your classroom is to give your students a sense of belonging. They need to see their photos all over the room: name cards with their picture on their cubby, on a name wall in the classroom, on practice cards in the writing center, on an attendance chart or check-in spot, etc. Students need to have a sense of ownership and belonging. They should feel like your classroom is a *family*. You want your classroom family to be one that fosters and builds a sense of safety and security for all students because they won't all have the opportunity to experience that at home. Another benefit of giving your students ownership in the classroom is that they end up taking better care of their space and the materials they use.

Another great goal to have in place is to make the content you're teaching fun and playful. It's truly the ultimate challenge because academic subjects aren't inherently fun or playful. At every turn, you can decide: What can I do to make this content more fun and playful than anything else that's going on in the classroom? You may incorporate songs, puppets, or three-dimensional objects. I liken play to "hiding the veggies in the mac and cheese." If there's a great mix of solid instruction (those veggies!) and playful experiences (the cheese!), your students are learning. The ultimate test of your effectiveness as a teacher is this: If your students go home at the end of the day and their parents ask what they learned that day, they should say, "I had fun! I played!" Early childhood education must be fun and playful to be effective.

A final foundational goal I will mention is creating an environment where your students want to come every day. They are happy and excited to get up in the morning. You know you're successful when parents call you on a holiday, telling you they had to break it to their child that there's no school and their child is having a full-blown meltdown. Their students simply won't accept that there is no school on a "regular" school day. That's when you know you've made it!

As you have already seen throughout this book, academic goals are important too, but they should be broken down into smaller, bite-sized goals that support the bigger picture. You will then be able to assess your students' progress and adjust your teaching as necessary, rather than waiting for the "ta-da!" moment at the end of the year when you finally discover whether your students are kindergarten ready or not. Once you have set specific goals, you will be able to create a plan.

HABIT TWO: CREATE A PLAN

To become a proactive teacher, you need to develop a plan *before* your students have reached the end of the plan you already have in place. The right plan is not built around the large-scale requirements of the by-the-end-of-the-year standards; you approach planning by starting at a smaller level, breaking down each one of the standards into its component pieces, step by step.

For example, if the standard you're teaching to is "Tracks print with 1:1 correspondence," an effective teacher will say, *I need to start the year with a plan in place that will walk my students step by step through how to handle a book.* If your students can't handle a book, they can't track the print in a book! Your students need to know things about books like: books have a cover, a back, how to turn the pages, when books are right side up vs. upside down, etc. It's true that some students will come to you with that knowledge already in place but be proactive on behalf of *all* your students. Use a tool like our "book handling skills" kit at Pre-K Pages. Set your students up for success.

For each standard you need to teach, develop a plan that breaks down that standard into the precursor skills that support it. And then? Don't just plan to teach the skill once, but give your students repeated exposure to that concept until you are certain that 100% of your students have mastered it. Don't forget to check the HEART method (explained in Chapter 5) when considering individual activities or lessons.

HABIT THREE: REFLECT

The third habit excellent teachers adopt is a habit of continuous reflection on what's going on in your classroom: with your lessons, in your centers, with your classroom culture, etc. If you're the "pen and paper" journaling type and already write down your thoughts each day, you likely reflect best in this way. However, reflection isn't just limited to writing or journaling. Sometimes my best times of reflection come when I least expect them, like in the shower, on my drive to and from school, or in the middle of the night. Just giving yourself regular space to "be" will open up opportunities for reflection. When your brain encounters unresolved problems, it naturally goes to work trying to solve them.

Reflecting also doesn't require complete stillness or isolation. You may be involved in creative pursuits like scrapbooking, watercolor painting, knitting, or horseback riding! Or you may simply be pausing to enjoy a cup of tea. Whichever method feels most natural to you, that's the one in which a habit of reflection will *stick*. Give yourself time and space where you're not rushed and not feeling pressured to move on to the next thing. Teachers deserve breaks, too! When you return from a reflection session—even if it's just for 10–15 minutes—you'll feel more rested, refreshed, and ready to tackle the next challenge to solve in your classroom.

HABIT FOUR: ADJUST

Once you start carving out time for regular reflection, the next habit comes naturally. If you recognize that there are unresolved issues coming up in your classroom, it is important to acknowledge the feeling of being "stuck." Sometimes, admitting this to yourself takes a lot of courage! You may be facing a situation where you feel stuck with respect to one child's development, or it may be that you are not meeting benchmarks you have established for your class. When that happens, it is time to investigate.

Before we talk about ways to investigate the underlying issues involved, though, it is also important to note that just because you're feeling frustrated doesn't always mean you are stuck. I have known teachers in the past who tended to make a mountain out of a molehill: their problems, once they started talking about them, turned out not to be significant in the grand scheme of things. There is a difference between actually being stuck and just hitting a small bump in the road, and it is possible that all you need is a healthy mindset shift to take the small things in stride and press on.

Once you have determined that the challenge you are facing is significant, it is time to investigate. What are the causes behind the problem? Does it have to do with you, or is it more about your classroom dynamics and the students themselves? Is it something you have control over, or is your ability to change the situation limited to simply being a positive *influence*, but the choices belong to other people? At times, you will also be faced with problems over which you have *no* control, and you must settle for changing those things that are in *your* power to change. This is where developing a relationship with a wise mentor comes in (which we will talk about next).

Once you have identified the true causes of the issues you are dealing with, you will want to decide how to incorporate your observations into the very next day's lessons. That is one reason it is so important to do your planning based on small, bite-sized foundational skills instead of huge yearlong goals. If you are working on teaching children a specific skill and they are hitting a roadblock, you can implement changes right away and not waste weeks of planning effort that turns out to be of little use.

HABIT FIVE: CONNECT

You may be surprised to discover that your biggest periods of growth as a teacher come at times when you are most connected to *other* teachers. There are hundreds of thousands of teachers, all over the country, who either have more experience than you do, or who come from a different background. These differences can make your mentors uniquely equipped to see what is really going on in your situation, objectively. Sometimes a simple word of encouragement or a recommended "first step" can spark the flame that will keep you moving forward and growing as an educator.

I will say it again: connection with a community of mentors is one of the most critical tools you can have in your toolbelt as a teacher. I know the intense isolation you can feel when you shut the doors to your own classroom and only interact with three- to five-year-olds for hours on end. A little time spent with other professional educators, even if it's in an online/virtual community, can help you feel less alone. The more connected you are, the more effective you will become as a teacher.

HEATHER'S SECRET RECIPE

It may be that you already have the necessary resources in the town or city where you live to put all these habits into practice. You may teach in a large Title I or Head Start program where you are surrounded by pre-K teachers all trying to move your students forward, together. You may work in a corporate childcare setting as part of a professional teaching team. If this is the case, you may already have access to the resources you need. In many cases, though, teachers find themselves isolated in their classrooms: they are either the only pre-K teacher in an elementary school, or they are in-home childcare providers, where they have little to no contact with adults other than their spouse and the parents of their students. This was the case with Heather, to whom I introduced you at the start of this chapter.

Three years ago, Heather was working as a solo provider in her at-home childcare center. She felt isolated and disconnected from any larger teaching community. She knew she wanted to excel as a teacher, and she often contacted local kindergarten teachers to help guide her in what was most important for her students to know by the time they left her class and graduated to local elementary schools. However, Heather knew that without the support of a pre-K community, she would be handicapped. She would not make the kind of progress she wanted to make as a professional educator, as she would have to rely on learning from her own mistakes. So how, in just three years, did Heather go from an overwhelmed, exhausted teacher, always second guessing herself, to a knowledgeable, confident pro?

Heather's "secret recipe" came in the form of joining an online pre-K curriculum, mentorship, and continuing education/professional development organization called the Teaching Trailblazers. She has been a long-time member (since 2017) because, she says, it's a "no brainer." She can get all the training she needs to keep her in-home childcare license in her state, and because the number of printable resources inside the Teacher Resource Vault have nearly doubled since she first joined the Trailblazers, she has almost limitless options. She told me at our meetup in Detroit that she will *always* be a member because it's not just the "same old same old"—the value of what she has access to in the Trailblazers continues to grow.

If Heather has questions or needs to talk to another in-home childcare provider, she knows exactly where to go to ask her burning questions. She can also connect with public school teachers to verify that she is on the right track and keeping pace with the standards. By attending the live office hours with her fellow teachers, she gets the chance to chat about different topics and learn from their experiences and insights. I am there too, to help teachers solve—once and for all—the problems they face in their classrooms.

Heather wants to be sure that her students leave her in-home childcare fully equipped to transition into kindergarten and be successful there. But she feels secure and confident, knowing she has a plan to follow and the absolute *best* at her fingertips.

Think back to the times you've been handed a "pre-K in a box" packaged curriculum. You spend hours—or days—sitting in the middle of your classroom, with piles of cute-but-ineffective paper all around you. You are stuck poring through the teacher's manual, trying to figure out a system for applying what's inside. Sometimes the contents of that box will be appropriate for your students, but sometimes it's not...which simply adds to your stress. And let's don't forget the nightmare of trying to figure out how to pack all those materials back *into* its packaging—it's like a jack in the box, ready to spring back out when you least expect it!

For more than 20 years I have been mentoring teachers online—via lesson plans, printable hands-on, play-based activities, and my blog at Pre-K Pages. Five years ago, I brought that mentoring to live in one single place, the Teaching Trailblazers. If you decide to join me there, all you must do is open your browser. We've already paved the way with everything you need to be an early childhood education success story.

Whether or not you decide to join me over at the Teaching Trailblazers, you can still become the teacher you have always dreamed of.

NEXT STEP: GET CONNECTED

Option 1: Explore the book companion site at https://www.pre-kpages.com/TeachSmarter for help getting started with teaching smarter, not harder when it comes to early literacy.

Here's what you'll find there:

Quick video tips to further clarify each of the four steps.

Printable resources to help you implement and embrace each step.

Challenges to help you gain confidence as you begin to make small changes to your teaching practice.

Links to additional resources to help deepen your understanding of each step.

Option 2: Get connected.

If you have access to a local community of early childhood educators, with whom you can share your frustrations and struggles, but also celebrate your victories, by all means, do it! Time spent in a teaching community should never be seen as "extra" or unnecessary. Instead, I would challenge you to view your relationships with other dedicated teachers as a critical component of your success. Find mentors. Get professional development training on *your* terms, in a format that makes sense for you and your busy life. Choose a curriculum that supports the best practices represented in the HEART method. Get creative. Pour into your students' social-emotional learning and *connect*.

If you do not have access to a local community of dedicated early childhood education peers who are committed to growing into their best selves as teachers, please know that I am here to support you. Via the Teaching Trailblazers, I am ready and waiting to propel you forward in your quest to become an outstanding teacher who makes a long-term difference in the lives of her students.

References

Anthony, J. L., Lonigan, C. J., Driscoll, K., Phillips, B. M., & Burgess, S. R. (2003). Phonological sensitivity: A quasi-parallel progression of word structure units and cognitive operations. *Reading Research Quarterly*, 38(4), 470–487.

Baker, J. M., & Jordan, K. E. (2015). The influence of multisensory cues on representation of quantity in children. In D. C. Geary, D. B. Berch, & K. M. Koepke (Eds.), *Mathematical cognition and learning. Vol. 1: Evolutionary origins and early development of number processing* (pp. 277–301). Elsevier.

Ball, E. W., & Blachman, B. A. (1991). Does phoneme awareness training in kindergarten make a difference in early word recognition and developmental spelling? *Reading Research Quarterly*, 26(1), 49–66.

Bryant, P. E., MacLean, M., Bradley, L. L., & Crossland, J. (1990). Rhyme and alliteration, phoneme detection, and learning to read. *Developmental Psychology*, 26(3), 429–438.

Byrne, B., & Fielding-Barnsley, R. (1989). Phonemic awareness and letter knowledge in the child's acquisition of the alphabetic principle. *Journal of Educational Psychology*, 81(3), 313–321.

Byrne, B., & Fielding-Barnsley, R. (1991). Evaluation of a program to teach phonemic awareness to young children. *Journal of Educational Psychology*, 83(4), 451–455.

Cassano, C., & Rohde, L. (2019). *Phonological awareness in early childhood literacy development* (Position Statement and Research Brief). International Reading Association. 10.13140/RG.2.2.16213.99041

Cassano, C. M., & Schickedanz, J. A. (2015). An examination of the relations between oral vocabulary and phonological awareness in early childhood. *Literacy Research: Theory, Method, and Practice*, 64(1), 227–248.

Clay, M. M. (2000). *Concepts about print: What have children learned about the way we print language?* Heinemann.

Collins, K., & Glover, M. (2015). *I am reading: Nurturing young children's meaning making and joyful engagement with any book*. Heinemann.

Covey, S. R., & Covey, S. (2020). *The 7 habits of highly effective people.* Simon & Schuster.

Dede, C. (2010). Comparing frameworks for 21st century skills. In J. A. Bellanca & R. S. Brandt (Eds.), *21st century skills: Rethinking how students learn* (pp. 51–76). Solution Tree Press.

Dickinson, D. K., & Neuman, S. B. (Eds.). (2007). *Handbook of early literacy research* (Vol. 2). Guilford Press.

Dickinson, D. K., & Tabors, P. O. (2001). *Beginning literacy with language: Young children learning at home and school.* Paul H Brookes Publishing.

Foulin, J. N. (2005). Why is letter-name knowledge such a good predictor of learning to read? *Reading and Writing*, 18(2), 129–155.

Fountas, I. C., & Pinnell, G. S. (2018). *Literacy beginnings: A prekindergarten handbook.* Heinemann.

Hunter, R. (2004). *Madeline Hunter's mastery teaching: Increasing instructional effectiveness in elementary and secondary schools* (2nd ed.). Corwin Press.

Jordan, K. E., & Baker, J. (2011). Multisensory information boosts numerical matching abilities in young children. *Developmental Science*, 14(2), 205–213.

Juel, C., & Leavell, J. A. (1988). Retention and nonretention of at-risk readers in first grade and their subsequent reading achievement. *Journal of Learning Disabilities*, 21(9), 571–580.

Kintsch, W. (2005). An overview of top-down and bottom-up effects in comprehension: The CI perspective. *Discourse Processes*, 39(2–3), 125–128.

Lesaux, N. K., & Harris, J. R. (2015). *Cultivating knowledge, building language: Literacy instruction for English learners in elementary school.* Heinemann.

Lonigan, C. J., Burgess, S. R., & Anthony, J. L. (2000). Development of emergent literacy and early reading skills in preschool children: Evidence from a latent-variable longitudinal study. *Developmental Psychology*, 36(5), 596–613.

Lonigan, C. J., Burgess, S. R., Anthony, J. L., & Barker, T. A. (1998). Development of phonological sensitivity in 2- to 5-year-old children. *Journal of Educational Psychology*, 90(2), 294–311.

McKenna, M. C., & Dougherty Stahl, K. A. (2009). *Assessment for reading instruction* (2nd ed.). Guilford Press.

National Early Literacy Panel. (2008). *Developing early literacy: Report of the National Early Literacy Panel.* National Institute for Literacy.

Neuman, S. B., & Wright, T. S. (2014). The magic of words: Teaching vocabulary in the early childhood classroom. *American Educator*, 38(2), 4–13.

Neumann, M. M., Hood, M., & Ford, R. M. (2013). Using environmental print to enhance emergent literacy and print motivation. *Reading and Writing*, 26(5), 771–793.

O'Connor, R. E., Jenkins, J. R., Leicester, N., & Slocum, T. A. (1993). Teaching phonological awareness to young children with learning disabilities. *Exceptional Children*, 59(6), 532–546.

Piasta, S. B., & Wagner, R. K. (2010). Developing early literacy skills: A meta-analysis of alphabet learning and instruction. *Reading Research Quarterly*, 45(1), 8–38.

Saville-Troike, M. (1988). Private speech: Evidence for second language learning strategies during the "silent" period. *Journal of Child Language*, 15(3), 567–590.

Sénéchal, M., Ouellette, G., Pagan, S., & Lever, R. (2012). The role of invented spelling on learning to read in low-phoneme awareness kindergartners: A randomized-control-trial study. *Reading and Writing*, 25(4), 917–934.

Snow, C. E., Burns, S. M., & Griffin, P. (Eds.). (1998). *Preventing reading difficulties in young children*. National Academy Press.

Spira, E. G., Bracken, S. S., & Fischel, J. E. (2005). Predicting improvement after first-grade reading difficulties: The effects of oral language, emergent literacy, and behavior skills. *Developmental Psychology*, 41(1), 225–234.

Stanovich, K. E., Cunningham, A. E., & Cramer, B. B. (1984). Assessing phonological awareness in kindergarten children: Issues of task comparability. *Journal of Experimental Child Psychology*, 38(2), 175–190.

Wells, G. (1986). *The meaning makers: Children learning language and using language to learn*. Heinemann.

Woodrome, S. E., & Johnson, K. E. (2009). The role of visual discrimination in the learning-to-read process. *Reading and Writing*, 22(2), 117–131.

Yopp, H. K. (1988). The validity and reliability of phonemic awareness tests. *Reading Research Quarterly*, 23(2), 159–177.

Yopp, H. K., & Yopp, R. H. (2000). Supporting phonemic awareness development in the classroom. *Reading Teacher*, 54(2), 130–143.

Index

Note: Page references in *italics* refer to figure and boxed text.

See also Challenge
  to change
  current teaching
  practice
Connection, 152–153, 155
  See also HEART guide in
    preparing lessons

D

Defeated feeling, over-
  coming, 135–138, *135*
Dual language learners,
  94, 115–116

E

Early childhood education,
  elevating field of,
  146
English as a second language
  students,
  94, 115–116
Environmental print, 62–63,
  63, 64, 65, 66

F

Flannel boards, 133–134, *133*

G

Goals, setting right, 148–150

H

Habits of excellent
  teachers:
  adjust, 157
  connect, 152–153
  create a plan, 150–151
  overview of, 146–148
  reflect, 41–43, 151
  set the right
    goals, 148–150
  *7 Habits of Highly
    Effective People*
    and, 147, *147*
Hands-on activities,
  99–102
  See also HEART guide in
    preparing
    lessons
HEART guide in pre-
  paring lessons:
  A Connection
    alphabet
      knowledge, 36, *37*
    oral lan-
      guage, 129–130
    phonological
      awareness,
      105–106
    print awareness, 70
  description of, 33–34
  Enticing

in context, 10–11
holes versus no holes,
    20
in isolation, 9–10, 24
letter-of-the-week
    practice,
    9–10, *11*,
    12–14, *12*, 17–19
motivation for, 21–22
with names of children,
    21–24, *25*, 26
order of teaching letters
    and, 23–24, *29*
recognizing letters and,
    26–27
sorting letters and, *20*, 21
sounds of letters, 91–92
uppercase versus
    lowercase letters
    and, 26–27, 29
visual discrimination and,
    19, *20*, 21
writing letters and, 26–27
See also Alpha-
    bet knowledge
Lisa case study, 135, 140–142
Literacy:
    complex process of, 7
    ingredients for, 7, 78–79
    oral language's
        role in, 114

reading process and, 67
research on, emergent, 12
resources for early, 155
Lowercase letters, 26–27, 29

M

Memorization:
    alphabet
        knowledge and, 4–6
    learning process of chil-
        dren and, 7
    of poem, 5–6
    rote, 4–7
Modeling behavior, 132–133
Motivation:
    for alphabet knowledge,
        learning, 7
    learning process
        and, 21–22
    for letter learning, 21–22
    for reading, 53–55, 62–63,
        63, *64*, *65*, 66
Multiple readings of same
    story, 67, 124–125,
    125, 132, 134

N

Name activities, 22
New policies on teaching,
    incorporating, 14–16

Print awareness:
  basic, 51–52
  belief in reading ability
    and, 55–56, 67–68
  challenge to change
    current teaching prac-
    tice and, 71
  class books and, cre-
    ating, 62, *63*
  differences of students
    learning, 49–51
  environmental print and,
    62–63, *63*, *64*, *65*,
    66
  HEART guide in preparing
    lessons for
      A Connection, 70
      Enticing, 69–70
      Hands-on, 69
      Repeated Exposure, 70
      Time for Prac-
      tice, 70–71
  importance of, 52–53
  motivation to read and,
    53–55, 62–63, *63*,
    64, *65*, 66
  overview of, 45
  pocket chart sentences
    and, *65*, *66*, 67, *68*
  precursors to, 53
  print concepts and, 52

  print-rich classroom envi-
    ronment and, *28*, 29
  reading big book with
    pointer and, 57–59, 67
  reading success and, 7
  reading time and,
    59, *60*, *61*
  reflection on,
    60–71, 69–71
  self-assessment of
    teaching, 72
  troubleshooting, 72–74
  uppercase and lowercase
    letters and, 27
  See also Books
Professional development
  training, 155
  See also Teaching Trail-
    blazers mentor-
    ship program
Puppet theater, 128,
  131–133, *131*

R

Reading:
  aloud, by child, 123–124
  alphabet knowledge and
    success in, 7
  belief in ability,
    55–56, 67–68

big book with
pointer, 57–59,
67
factors determining
success in, 7
literacy and process of, 67
motivation for, 53–55,
62–63, *63*, *64*, *65*,
66
pocket chart sentences
and, *65*, *66*, 67, *68*
print awareness and
success in, 7
time for in classroom,
59, *60*, *61*
See also Books; Print
awareness
Reflection:
on alphabet
knowledge, 41–45
change and, 43, 45
growth as teacher and, 74
as habit of excellent
teachers, 41–43,
151
impact of, 41–43, 151
importance of, 41
on oral language, 130–131
on phonological aware-
ness, 108–110
on print awareness, 69–71

self-assessment and, 44
Regulation skills of children,
teaching, 118, 122
Rhyming, 80, 93–94

S

Scaffolding, 122, *122*
Self-assessment of teaching:
alphabet knowledge, 44
oral language, 131
phonological
awareness, 109
print awareness, 72
Self-regulation skills of
children,
118, 122
Sentence segmentation, 80
Social skills of children,
teaching, 118, 122
Songs, 96–97
Sorting letters, *20*, 21
Sound word discrim-
ination, 80
Sounds of letters,
learning, 91–92
Storytelling center, 128–133
Syllable blending and
deletion, 80
Syllable instruction, 99–101,
109–110, *109*

T

Teaching Trailblazers
mentorship
program:
  burnout man-
    agement and,
    140–142, *140, 141*
  case studies
    AnneMarie, 135–138
    Jennifer, 135, 138–140
    Lisa, 135, 140–142
    overview of, 135
  challenge to
    change current
    practice and, *102*
  defeated feeling
    and, overcoming,
    135–138, *135*
  Heather case study
    growth as teacher
      by, 143–145
    success recipe
      of, 153–154
  impact of, on
    teaching, 136–137
  lesson planning ideas
    and, 138–140
  self-regulation/social skills
    and, 118, 122

  supportive community
    of, xv, 8, 19, *102,
    137,* 154–155
  teaching resources, *137,*
    139–140, *140,* 141,
    141
Teaching versus telling, 29
Troubleshooting:
  alphabet
    knowledge, 44–45,
    44
  oral language, 131–134
  phonological awareness,
    109–110
  print awareness, 72–74

U

Uppercase letters, 26–27, 29

V

Visual discrimination,
  19, *20,* 21
Vocabulary development,
  122–123, *122, 123*

W

Wordless picture books,
  123–124, *124*